Milly's Story

*A Young Girl's Memories of
the Second World War
Luxembourg 1940 - 1945*

Milly Thill

"Milly's Story: A Young Girl's Memories of the Second World War, Luxembourg 1940 – 1945," by Milly Thill. ISBN 1-58939-536-0.

Published 2004 by Virtualbookworm.com Publishing Inc., P.O. Box 9949, College Station, TX , 77842, US. ©2004 Milly Thill. All rights reserved. No part of this publication may be reproduced, stored in a retrieval system, or transmitted in any form or by any means, electronic, mechanical, recording or otherwise, without the prior written permission of Milly Thill.

Printed in the United States of America.

Milly's Story

A Young Girl's Memories of
the Second World War
Luxembourg 1940 - 1945

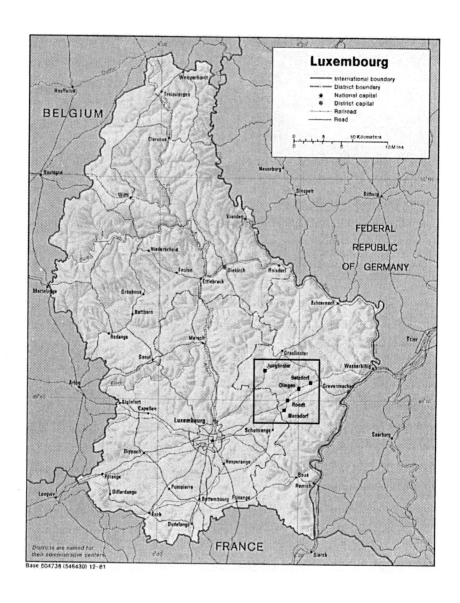

Luxembourg

- ━━━━━━ International boundary
- ┄┄┄┄┄ District boundary
- ★ National capital
- ⊛ District capital
- ┈┈┈┈┈ Railroad
- ━━━━━ Road

0 ___ 5 ___ 10 Kilometers
0 ___ 5 ___ 10 Miles

BELGIUM

FEDERAL

REPUBLIC

OF GERMANY

Hauffaize
Wemperhardt
Troisvierges
Bastogne
Clervaux
Nauerburg
Wiltz
Sinspert
Bitburg
Vianden
Niederscheid
Feulen
Diekirch
Reisdorf
Ettelbruck
Echternach
Grosbous
Bettborn
Trier
Redange
Mersch
Martelange
Bissel
Graulinster
Junglinster
Wasserbillig
Setzdorf
Olingen
Grevenmacher
Siegenfort
Capellen
Roodt
Mensdorf
Luxembourg
Schuttrange
Saarburg
Bippach
Hesperange
Bous
Remich
Potange
Differdange
Longwy
Pontpierre
Bettembourg
Fysange
Esch
Dudelange
Siorck

FRANCE

Districts are named for
their administrative centers

Base 504738 (546430) 12-81

Contents

PREFACE

By John E. Dolibois

OLINGEN IS LOCATED just a short kilometer north of the main road from Luxembourg City to Grevenmacher on the German border. I know the little village on the Syr river well. My schoolmate and best friend, Albert Stoltz, lived on the route de Flaxweiler until his death two years ago. Albert and his wife, Marguerite, hosted my wife, Winnie, and me on many pleasant occasions. Just a stone's throw from my friend's house is the railroad crossing, which is mentioned frequently in Milly's reminiscences of the Second World War. The road from Betzdorf to Roodt-sur-Syr runs parallel to the river and the railway tracks.

I have hiked up the 'Kéisberg' for a good look at the valley of the Syr, and I well remember the pungent odour of the rich manure piles in front of the farmhouses of Olingen. In driving to Betzdorf for a Boy Scout Jubica one day in 1982, I narrowly missed a cow which had strayed into the road just about the time I came along. I was the United States Ambassador to Luxembourg at the time. It would have been a tragic comedy for a superpower's envoy to have bashed a harmless but stupid bovine on the main street of Olingen.

I was born in Luxembourg, emigrated to the United States as a boy and returned 50 years later as America's representative to my native country. And as a boy I had often travelled through Olingen by train to Echternach to visit that charming city or to spend a holiday in the surrounding 'Muellerthal,' the Little Switzerland' of Luxembourg.

During the Second World War I was stationed in Luxembourg for a while, and often drove around the area of Milly's memoirs to witness the devastation war had wrought. I saw first hand the results of the fighting between the German invaders and the American liberators. My Embassy years, and the subsequent visits to the Grand Duchy, often brought me to the valley of the Syr to visit friends in Mensdorf, Uebersyren, Roodt and Olingen.

That is why, when I first read Milly's story, I felt carried back 60 years, 50 years and 10 years, remembering as a walked where I used to run.

Some readers of this book may not be led to such glimmers from the past, as I was, but he or she can be prepared for a good read. One first thinks, with some regret, that the memoirs of a young girl in a small village would be of interest only to Luxembourgers who shared similar experiences, and maybe only to readers who know the area, the language and the circumstances. But long before finishing the final page, one will conclude that this story has appeal for anyone who wants to get a first-hand look at life under Nazi occupation as experienced by a young girl . . . not to mention the thrill of liberation after four years of stress and horror.

Thousands of German troops, the invaders, passed through Olingen on that fateful 10th of May 1940. One of them vaguely replied to Milly's father, who asked 'Where did you enter our country?' by saying: 'It doesn't matter; what lies behind us is over . . . we strive only forward.' The metal buckle of his belt was inscribed 'Gott Mit Uns.' Milly and her family saw them come, and then saw them leave four years later – in retreat. God was with them for only a short time.

Readers who want to know 'when good merchandise becomes rare' will read all about it in Milly's story, at times shaking their heads in disbelief and at other times chuckling in amusement. The German Gauleiter's bureaucracy administered food stamps and, unwittingly, encouraged black marketeering. The Luxembourgers understood how to tighten their belts; they exercised good humour, with many a laugh behind the Germans' backs.

The German soldiers looted and the bureaucrats administered – interfering with church and school. The Gestapo threatened and punished. Trains were derailed, and schoolmasters and priests arrested. Life was never easy during those occupation years. The readers of this story will learn how to make soap, raise rabbits and chickens and how to slaughter on the sly. There are recollections of a weightless pig's head and of a pig with two tails.

The miller of Olingen was a 'smart guy,' according to Milly. He knew his trade and how to hide 'the English' in his mill. The much hated German rulers could not dampen the spirits of determined Olingers, who made their Octave pilgrimage during the occupation despite the Germans' efforts to thwart them. How to cope with false German propaganda and how to help friends in need when German inspectors made it almost impossible? Milly's story provides the answers, with humor and with tears, with courage and stubbornness, a Luxembourg characteristic.

Finally, the story of the Liberation in September 1944. 'The Americans are here!' Just in time for a Christmas they will never forget – not the people from the small village of Olingen, not the Americans from far away – ever. How can a village of 200 inhabitants cope with housing one thousand GIs? They managed, and were able to care for evacuees from border towns to boot. Such problems 'added ever more solemnity to the traditional Christmas Eve services.'

The 'mouth-watering smell of fried eggs and bacon' made the people of Olingen forget the icy winter air. After years of suffering under the occupiers' regime, they now worried about the GIs whose daily missions took them into headlong combat during the infamous Battle of the Bulge. Would their liberators return safely to their billets at nightfall? Some did not. And those who survived to fight another day were grateful for the apple pies baked by Milly's mother, for the warming 'Schnaaps' served by her father, while they 'gambled' a 'sixty-six' at cards for relaxation.

Milly's memoirs are flavoured with chocolate and chewing gum, which turned up in abundance. She relates stories of US Army waste, the sometimes reckless abandon of equipment, combined with typical GI disregard for their hosts' furniture and other belongings. Her tales present, fairly, a series of incidents of life with American soldiers billeted in private homes, who give much and take little. By contrast, the German occupiers had taken everything and given nothing.

Milly's story ends with her account of participation in the historic Echternach jumping procession.. This centuries-old event is held in honor of St Willibrord, who founded an abbey in Echternach in the 7th century. The dancing procession is unique in the world. Thousands of pilgrims and tourist visitors from all over Luxembourg and neighboring countries take part in this religious ritual.

In 1945 it had a special meaning for Milly. It took place in the city on the German border, which was hardest hit by the fighting, with more than 60 per cent destruction. The basilica, holding the crypt of St Willibrord, lay in ruins. While the Olingen people would never forget the war years, the bitter memories did not prevent them from celebrating the traditional Pentecost festival in their customary style. The difficult years in the valley of the Syr were coming to an end for Milly, the teller of tales. 'Whatever lay behind was over . . . . .' She was now to strive only forward, driven by her determination to become a successful teacher, an ambition she was richly to fulfill.

Milly's story is timely historical contribution to her nation, a tribute to the people of Luxembourg for their courage and fortitude during the terrible years of Nazi occupation, as well as to their brave young American liberators. It should also be of particular interest to everyone that lived through that war or took part in it, to American citizens of Luxembourg descent or to anyone curious to know what it was like to live in a small country under Nazi rule in German-occupied territory at that time.

John E. Dolibois
US Ambassador to Luxembourg 1981-1985
Vice-President Emeritus, Miami University, Oxford, Ohio

FOREWORD
By Edward M. Rowell

WAR IS AN INTENSELY personal tragedy. The abstractions of history books, the distortions of film fantasies, even the benumbing flood of modern television images somehow fail to penetrate our inner lives. But all wars ultimately consist of individual experiences. That is the truth and value of these reminiscences from a war of 50 years ago whose horror remains contemporary in our day.

In these essays a young girl, Milly, makes us feel, see, hear, smell and taste reality. We experience humanity and inhumanity, fear and fleeting moments of laughter, deprivation and danger, courage and resilience. The stories are true. The people are real. It is a good read.

Edward M. Rowell
United States Ambassador to Luxembourg, 1990-1994.

PREFACE
By Jul Christophory

I DO NOT KNOW whether to consider myself lucky – or rather feel jealous - for having shared only some of the experiences suffered by Milly Thill during the five years of World War II in Luxembourg.

The fact is that I delved into her book with great interest in order to find out how the diffuse memories of a five-year old farm boy – in 1944 – overlap with her first-hand account of a village girl who must have been born nine years earlier. So she had the questionable privilege to consciously witness the whole plot of the second drama of the 20th century, whereas I got only involved in the final act of a thundering tank battle preceding the joyful liberation of the city of Luxembourg by the American GIs in September 1944. I have described the details of these events elsewhere.[1]

No wonder then that most of her chapters deal with comic or tragic features of the German occupation in her home village. She saw "them" come, stay and leave in a frantic retreat in the early September days of 1944.

Her most captivating anecdotes illustrate the resourceful resistance the Luxembourg villages opposed to the new regime

---

[1] Cf. e.g. « The Liberty Road in the Grand Duchy of Luxembourg 1944-1994 Imprimerie St Paul 1994 pp. 81-86

and describe the way they managed to survive and to keep their own identity in difficult circumstances.

My perspective of those early war years was of course a different one.

Living on an isolated farm, under the full control of the German army which had established its technical supply, maintenance and repair unit for military vehicles in the shadow of the tall orchard trees of the near-by castle of Grevels, it was of course more difficult for my parents to operate on the sly and to beat German bureaucracy. And yet Milly Thill's tales about those days trigger off so many deeply-buried and seemingly forgotten events with their particular flavour and sensation, like the official or secret slaughtering of pigs and calves accompanied by the necessary double-talk or secrecies in front of German officials or Luxembourg nazi supporters and collaborators.

The fairly regular weekend visits of friends and acquaintances from the city coming to the farm in order to provide themselves with some decent extra-food and thus keep up their normal gastronomic standards in spite of an insufficient number of food ration stamps allocated to them. Whether you call it black marketeering or hoarding ("Hamstern") this phenomenon is surely one of the outstanding recollections of those days.

I also recall the excitement we felt as children at the sight of the shiny uniforms of the German officers, their technical equipment and gigantic vehicles like armoured trucks, patrol cars, field kitchens etc. It was an eerie world we were allowed to enter. We little knew about its destructive capacity to wreak havoc on innocent people and to destroy the architectural heritage of our homeland.

Concerning the episode of the liberation by the Americans, I can of course fully testify to the accuracy of Milly Thill's report.

Although 9th September involved my family into the tragic event of a tank battle, which eventually led to the destruction of our farm, we still could save our lives and so enjoy in the following months and years the general revival and renewal of the country.

The contact with the American officers and the positive experience of the Marshall plan sparked off a miraculous enthusiasm for this unknown country whose boys had sacrificed their lives to liberate us. This thrill was to last for my whole professional career in which the contacts with American literature and civilisation and the English language always ranked foremost.

My teaching period at Miami University since the late sixties and my regular correspondence with two of our liberators, former US lieutenants James Newcomer (who was to devote many essays and a whole history-book in English to our country) and Martain Pietz (who was the commander of the first American tank being attacked by German shell-fire when approaching "Grevels-barrière" and thus one of the many heroes of the tank battle of September 9th on the eve of the liberation of Luxembourg-city) corroborated this basic sympathy.

Many a chapter of Milly Thill's reports is full of this delightful discovery in 1944 of the exotic flavour of genuine Army chocolate and chewing gum rations, the multitude and variety of canned food products like corned beef, the soft and juicy taste of mythic bananas and oranges which all of a sudden intruded into our dreary and monotonous eating habits, but also of our astonishment and bewilderment at some less pleasant aspects of the American way of life with its wilful waste and casual disregard for their hosts' furniture and belongings, in short at new economic concepts, new gastronomic and cultural standards and attitudes.

To the people of my generation I can only recommend these well-observed snapshots of the two sides of World War II in an occupied territory, expressed in a naïve, but alert and humorous way through the eyes of a child.

They will bring back both pleasant and less pleasant sensations, fears and hopes, both heroic and less heroic acts and thoughts.

To the younger ones, these pages may be a useful reminder of the disastrous consequences any new fanatical, sectarian and power-hungry political leader may bring about.......

Jul Christophory
Directeur de la Représentation / Commission
Européenne/Représentation au Luxembourg

Milly's Acknowledgments

"Milly's Story" is the translated version of the second part of her book "From the other bank of the Syr creek." This publication in Luxembourgish quickly became a bestseller.

Being a fan of the USA, Milly started to publish her personal war-memories in 1984 for the 40th anniversary celebration of her country's Liberation. In addition to this translation she pursued the publication in "Living in Luxembourg" issued by the American Women Club of Luxembourg. The enthusiastic reception shown especially at former GIs and at "Luxembourg Heritage" in the American mid-west encouraged her to translate in English the whole war-episode, from 1940 to 1945.

The author and her Luxembourgish readers would experience heartfelt joy if "Milly's Story" could earn the same fame and success from English speaking readers.

Milly owes special thanks to the supporters from the word "go," in particular:

- To Mr. Roland Gaul, former PR-manager at the US Embassy in Luxembourg
- To Mrs. Anny Faulk from the AWCL
- To Mrs. Larue Hall from Lynx Productions
- To Mr. Paul Meyers for his financial consulting support

Deep thanks for the different forewords written by:

- Mr. John E. Dolibois, US Ambassador to Luxembourg 1981-1985
- Mr. Edward M. Rowell, US Ambassador to Luxembourg 1990 -1994
- Mr. Jul Christophory, Director of the Representation / EU-Commission / Luxembourg

Profound gratitude is expressed to:

- Mr. Laurie Baillie for his excellent final touches given to the translation
- Mr. Bryan Kinnamon, Goodyear Akron in cooperation with
- Mr. Fernand Pletschette, Goodyear Luxembourg and his son André
- Mr. Jacques Roth for his efficient, animated and tireless computer assistance
- Mr. and Mrs. Louis & Elisa Evangelista for their perceptive advice and encouragement
- Mr. Scott Malensek, the U.S. author colleague, for his efficient recommendation of Virtualbookworm.com Publishing Inc.
- Mr. and Mrs. Jerry & Cynthia Brubaker for their useful recommendation concerning publication-engagements
- Mrs. Suzanne Bunkers, professor at Minnesota State University, for her precious help in searching for a publisher
- Many members of the American Women Club Luxembourg (AWCL) for their interest, valuable hints and encouragements.

Milly expresses honest thanks:

- To SES-GLOBAL L-6815 *Château de Betzdorf Luxembourg*

- To the MINISTERE DE LA CULTURE, DE L'ENSEIGNEMENT SUPERIEUR ET DE LA RECHERCHE of the *Ministry of Culture Luxembourg*
- To the FONDS CULTUREL NATIONAL of the *Ministry of Culture Luxembourg*

for their generous financial sponsoring.

As Luxembourg celebrates in 2004 the 60th Anniversary of Liberation, "Milly's Story" is especially dedicated to all the American soldiers who fought in the Grand Duchy of Luxembourg for the liberty of the nation during the Second World War and to the numerous descendants of the Luxembourgish emigrants to the USA.

In deep gratitude
Milly Thill

Drawing: Milly Thill

01 THE PRUSSIANS ARE COMING

THE ENTIRE VILLAGE OF OLINGEN was still asleep on that fateful Friday morning of the 10th of May 1940 when mother started her daily routine at a quarter past four. Life was hard for a railway signalman's wife in those days. They had to share their husband's duties as well as look after the station house where the family lived beside the level crossing. As usual she reported by phone to the Roodt railway station to let them know she was on duty. Around five thirty the first goods train from Roodt passed by. The first regular passenger train, known to the locals as the 'Bommeler' (the Dawdler), was due to arrive from Wasserbillig on the Moselle, the river separating Luxembourg from Germany.

But this morning the train, normally on time, was late. My mother received a call from the station at Wecker to tell her the train had not yet left Wasserbillig station. The caller added that the telephone lines seemed to have been interrupted. Mother hurried up to the bedroom, where dad was still sleeping, and woke him up to tell him what had happened. Their loud voices woke me up and I listened to their excited conversation. They were confused. Neither of them had the vaguest idea what was going on.

The phone rang again. On the line this time was the Wecker stationmaster, who made a general announcement to all the stations on the line from Wasserbillig to Luxembourg city that the German army had crossed the border at Wasserbillig and entered Luxembourg. He said the normal schedule would be disrupted but all station staff should remain on duty and be prepared for whatever might occur.

Mother rushed upstairs again, but this time with the awful news. Dad got out of bed at once and stood there in a state of shock. 'Damn! This means war.' A moment later I jumped out of bed too, opened the window and looked outside. 'What's going on? Where is the war?' I still remember how puzzled I was. There was nothing special to see or hear.

The sky was bright and clear. The sun had just risen over the forest and was sending its first golden rays into my bedroom. Everything was bathed in a deep, almost uncanny stillness. Not a living soul moved. Not a dog barked. Only our neighbor's rooster crowed while a bird twittered here and there in the orchards round our house and a fresh May scent wafted into my room. There was not a hint of war in the air.

Suddenly my mother came into the bedroom and told me that the Prussians, as we usually called the Germans, had invaded our country. 'What does that mean?' I asked, very frightened. She didn't reply. She just told me to stay in bed. I obeyed, but was much too excited to go back to sleep.

Mother and father then went downstairs. She put the coffee pot on the kitchen stove and he went to the laundry house for his morning toilet and shave. All of a sudden we heard a terrible noise from a distance. Dad shouted: 'Marguerite, Marguerite, come quickly. There they are – the Prussians are here.'

Mom rushed to the front of the house, where dad was pointing up to the sky, while I jumped out of bed and stuck my head out of the window. 'Jesus, Mary and Joseph!' mom cried. The sky was black with what looked like giant grasshoppers, which seemed to be swooping down on us, one after the other, coming from Betzdorf along the railway and the old Trier road, straight in the direction of our house.

'Mom, mom!' I screamed. My five-year-old brother, Marcel, rushed into my bedroom and started to scream along with me. The monsters approached and passed right over us, making a terrific noise and shaking the whole house. The windows rattled and the level crossing gates trembled. I crouched behind the corner closet while my brother jumped into my bed and hid under the covers. Mom rushed upstairs to protect us, shouting something about 'Prussian airplanes.'

As the deafening noise died away, mom and I looked out of the window. Dad was standing near the corner of the house and our neighbor the grocer on the other side of the railway line in front of his shop. His sister Lucy shot her head out of the window and back again twice as quickly, slamming the window shut as she did so, performing the whole operation in almost one movement. But she was not alone. We were all scared to death.

Drawing: Milly Thill

A little later came a second wave of those frightening-looking planes (today I realize they were the famous 'Stukas'). They were flying in the same direction as the first wave, straight over our house and very low. They even had to fly up and over the telephone line on the other side of our street. We could clearly see the heads of the pilots and the soldiers in the planes. As before, noise thundered all round us. I put my fingers in my ears and hid behind my mother while Marcel dived back under the sheets. They came and they came, wave after wave of these 'black crows,' as the massive airborne invasion continued to build up.

Finally, after about a quarter of an hour, it all seemed to be over. But everyone still felt very anxious, and my father and two of our neighbors, Jang and Jemp, got into a lively conversation about it all outside our house, wondering what lay behind the violation of this neutral country of ours. Only dad seemed to realize exactly what was happening: 'Those planes carrying the Prussian soldiers are preparing to occupy our country.' He was right.

Mother stayed inside with us children. She told us to put on our Sunday clothes as we would probably have to be evacuated. She started to pack clothes and underwear into a large suitcase and then went to get our new passports and tied them round our necks with string. When I asked her once more what would happen to us in this war, tears came into her eyes and she told us to pray. Later, when I got ready for early mass and school as usual, she insisted that I stay home that day.

When dad tried to phone the Roodt station for more information, the line went dead. Typical Prussian tactics, he said, stopping the flow of news and keeping us in the dark.

Then the man next door came into our house shouting that motorcycles and all sorts of vehicles were coming up the old Trier road. Uncle Jemp, as we children called my father's friend, then ran off along the ditch, the shortest cut to his house. Our other neighbor, Jang, disappeared too. Everyone seemed to be in a panic. Mom, dad, Marcel and I found ourselves left standing alone at the window, staring in disbelief as a whole division of soldiers on motor cycles with sidecars bore down upon our village at full speed.

They stopped at the level crossing and studied the maps they had hanging round their necks. Jesus, how ugly those Prussians looked, I thought, in their long gray-green overcoats, their bucket helmets and their oversized motorcycle goggles. Then they continued on their way, using a rural path behind our house.

Suddenly there was a banging on the door and to my horror one of them stepped into the house, his rifle over his shoulder. We all froze. I almost wet my pants. My brother ran to my mother and started screaming in fear, so she took him into the living room and shut the door behind her.

The German then approached dad and asked for the local authority. For a second dad was lost for words, but he eventually managed to blurt out: ' The village authority? That's our priest.' Now it was the soldier's turn to be taken aback: ' What, a parson!' he replied, almost contemptuously.

By this time my father had managed to recover his wits and replied in Luxembourgish: 'Ay, the community alderman, Jampir Buurg.' Dad then left the kitchen with the German and, from the doorway, pointed out the alderman's house and told him how to get there. The German thanked him, got back on his bike and roared off over the Syr bridge to the home of the alderman.

Mother then returned with my brother, still scared and still crying. I tried to comfort him while she and dad talked. Mum looked worried as dad told her how he'd been taken by surprise and had made a fool of himself by giving the German a stupid answer: 'What will become of us?' she wailed. 'The devil only knows,' dad replied.

Dad wanted to call on our neighbors on the other side of the creek, the Wagners, to find out what they knew about the situation. They were the only people in the village who had a radio at that time and dad was hoping to get some news from them. But mom didn't want him to leave the house, feeling that something was about to happen – and she was right.

Suddenly two soldiers came down the track in a railway car, which they braked just outside our house. They looked straight in at us, unsmiling and holding their rifles as though ready to shoot. But dad and mom remained calm, while Marcel and I ran helter-skelter into the house. Then, to our great relief, they carried on in the direction of Roodt.

Shortly after, another neighbor called my dad. He said German troops were pouring down the road from Betzdorf. From my window I could see them, a long moving caravan of vehicles and troops. Dad joined me. He swore softly: 'Damn it! What will become of us?'

At that moment mom let out a piercing scream from outside the house. We looked down and saw her pointing towards the Old Trier road, which was packed with columns of German troops, the cavalrymen looking so unfriendly with their helmets tightly fastened by leather straps under their chins. 'Jesus, Jesus!' she cried.

Soon the entire force arrived at the level crossing and moments later were swarming over the entire village. Olingen was occupied.

More German troops soon followed, all of them coming down the Old Trier road. We wondered who had told them about this road, which was little more than a track across fields and woods.

Around 8 o'clock the mechanized infantry passed the first house in Olingen. Very soon the whole village was alive with soldiers, horses, trucks, artillery pieces, anti-aircraft guns, field kitchen and Red Cross vans. Thousands of German troops passed through Olingen on that unforgettable day in May 1940.

Around noon, shortly after another column had come from a different direction and joined the other troops at the heart of the village, a soldier rushed right into our kitchen. Without a word he filled up his canteen with tap water. We all stared at him in astonishment, at his field-gray uniform, his knee-high leather jackboots and his heavy steel helmet.

Dad dared to ask him when and where they had entered the country. All he received in return was a curt and arrogant reply: ' Whatever lies behind us is over. We strive only forward.'

Then on the metal buckle of his belt I caught sight of wording 'Gott Mit Uns' which means 'God is with us.'

02 COMING OF THE 'LOCUSTS'

AFTER THE INITIAL SHOCK of the German invasion in May 1940, Luxembourgers soon grew to resign themselves to their fate. We almost got used to the unending columns of German soldiers, accompanied by a virtual caravan of troops on horseback or on motor-cycles with sidecars, flags and artillery guns, field kitchens and Red Cross vans, passing by for days on end, jamming the Luxembourg roads in the direction of Belgium and France.

Miles-long infantry columns marched in close order through Olingen too. The soldiers swung their arms and legs in time and sang loudly on command, as though from a single mouth, harsh German marching songs that grated in our heads. I still remember that triumphant chorus which echoed throughout our village: 'We march, we march, forever forward against England.'

May that year was particularly nice, warm and sunny. The village folk looked glum. They were standing or sitting in front of their houses idly watching the German columns marching and roaring by. The war they had been dreading for years had come to pass and our country had been invaded.

All normal activity had ceased and nobody was going to work. The radio and the press had been silenced and the telephone lines cut off. With no news of what was happening, we were completely in the dark.

To add to our confusion, rumors were circulating that our Government and our Grand Duchess Charlotte had fled the country and were somewhere in France. We couldn't believe it. Whatever were we going to do? What would happen to us?

A few days later we had to accept the bitter truth. We were under the heel of the Nazis and German forces were advancing on all fronts. It was a terrible shock.

Everybody began to prepare for the worse, but many people still put their faith in our neighbor France. The French army, they were convinced, would surely defeat the Germans and drive them back where they came from.

But then another gloomy scenario haunted our minds – war would rage across our country and we would all be evacuated. I still remember the fear I felt as a child as I heard all the stories being told of what such an upheaval would entail. I was only too keenly aware of the two big suitcases readily packed in our living room. I knew too that the new passport photos we had taken the previous month in anticipation of such an emergency were to be worn round our necks in case we got lost in the blind panic of an evacuation.

The mere thought of it froze me with fear and gave me some terrible nightmares. All children have a primeval fear of losing their parents and during those awful early days I never left my parents' side. What's more, I was terrified of the German soldiers. They looked so hard and cruel in their field-gray uniforms, their high boots, heavy helmets and long rifles.

In the village at Zirden's meadow, the German army had set up their field kitchen, where several different companies took their break round about noon. It wasn't long before all my school friends had gathered there to gaze at them, as children always do. Including me, for I soon joined them, even though I was a little nervous at first. We were quite amazed at what we saw.

The soldiers stood in long lines, carrying mess tins in which they were served a kind of stew. Then they collected in small groups in the meadow, along the creek, especially in the shadow of the trees, and even in Zirden's barn, which was filled with straw. They all seemed to be enjoying themselves, eating very rapidly, while talking and laughing at the same time. Some of them slipped off away from the crowd and took a quiet nap.

We were all ears, trying to catch every word, but could only pick up single words here and there. It was all so very different from what we had expected. They looked completely relaxed. They had dropped their rifles and their cartridge belts on the ground around them and had taken off their helmets, which enabled us to see how young and handsome many of them were.

My goodness, how different they looked without their helmets and weapons! I must admit they seemed to us to be very human — just nice ordinary boys having a good time and joking with their comrades.

Many of the soldiers had taken their boots off and were lying down to have the blisters on their feet seen to by the medical orderlies, whom we could recognize from the white bands with red crosses round their arms. While they were preparing the soldiers' feet for the long marches ahead they were joking and chatting away happily to them. Who would have thought this was an invading army!

The nearby public laundry house was another focal point of frenzied activity. Lots of soldiers were filling their canteens and splashing themselves with fresh water.

At Buurg's blacksmith's forge it was the turn of the horses to be fussed over. They were being brushed and groomed while drinking out of the stone basins and many of them were being given the smithy's traditional service of new horseshoes. Finally they had oat sacks hung round their necks and began to neigh loudly in appreciation.

The shouting of soldiers and the neighing of horses, not to speak of their smell, pervaded the entire village. It was bedlam.

But no one could really complain about any of that. Apart from making a lot of noise they were simply having a good time, as young soldiers do when a war is going their way.

What followed later, however, is another story and certainly gave all of us cause for complaint. The trouble started during the noon rest times and in the evenings, when the soldiers quartered in the houses and barns invaded the village groceries and emptied them of their entire stock.

From the front of our house, we watched them leaving Knuppen's grocery and drapery stores with large paper bags filled with coffee, sugar, chocolate, flour, toilet soap, tobacco, cigarettes and just about 'everything but the kitchen sink'! Even wool, cotton, thread and needles, underwear and fabric were borne away by the locust horde.

The perfume known as 'Soir de Paris' was in great demand, not of course for themselves but, via the field post, for their wives, girl friends and 'Mutties' (which, in German, means both mothers and grannies) back in Germany. And to rub it in they paid in our own Luxembourg currency. We were gob-smacked!

Drawing: Vito Lombardi

Within a matter of days the Germans had emptied our shops before we had a chance to react and grab what was left for ourselves. By the time the village housewives realized what had happened and rushed to the shops in a panic it was too late.

At Knuppen's, Cecile's and even the tiny Molleng's grocery, all the shelves were almost empty. Mom was terribly upset. She had wanted to do some shopping herself but had changed her mind when she remembered we could be evacuated. If that happened, it would be far better to have cash in our pockets than food left to rot away in our cupboards at home. We couldn't have taken it all with us.

Now it was too late anyway. A 'swarm of locusts' had descended on the village and cleaned it out.

Dad at once jumped on his bike and cycled to the next village, Roodt-Syr, but to no avail. At all the grocery stores, Lisa Gaffinet's, Binas's and even Jacob's, the largest, it was the same story. People were queuing up in front of the counters, many of them for nothing as the remaining goods were being sold only to regular customers.

Even they had to be satisfied with a liter of olive oil, a pound of coffee, a kilogram of sugar, a bar or two of soap and a few packets of cigarettes and tobacco. The groceries believed the wholesalers would turn up in the next few days and bring them fresh supplies of goods and produce, but they were wrong. Nothing came and the shops became emptier and emptier.

In the meantime the first evacuees were arriving in Olingen from the south of our country, the town of Bettembourg and the village of Elwingen, near Mondorf, both of which had been heavily shelled by French artillery. The inhabitants had to flee to save their lives.

They told us that Luxembourg's second largest town, Esch-sur-Alzette, and the neighboring town of Dudelange had been badly damaged by French shellfire but most of the locals had managed to escape to France.

Within a matter of days most of the houses in our beleaguered village were packed with German soldiers and Luxembourg evacuees, with hungry families having to cook their food in one kitchen.

By and large it worked out well, with most Luxembourg families making the best of a bad job and accepting the sacrifices that had to be made under wartime conditions, but disagreements inevitably arose and some people just couldn't get on together and parted on very bad terms.

On the other hand those days of upheaval and distress were not without their brighter side, for us children at least. We enjoyed countless happy hours and adventures in the company of the evacuated children and made many new friends among them. They taught us some exciting new games and we always managed to find some small corner of a garden or piece of meadow in which to play together.

One evening a gang of us climbed on to a bench beside the window of a house lodging a small detachment of German soldiers. As we spied into the living room — unobserved, we thought — we saw Hans, Klaus, Hermann and Peter shaving. We were giggling quietly among ourselves when suddenly one of the young Germans turned and pushed his soapy brush into the face of one of our gang. We all shrieked with laughter, including the German boys. Even the blackest times have their brighter moments.

They then made up for their joke by generously offering us some of the gray-black slices of 'Kamess' army bread and blood sausages lying on the table for their supper. At first we hesitated, but as they insisted and we were hungry, we quickly gobbled them down.

I cringe even now as I remember how it smelt and tasted. It was the first time I had tasted Kamess bread and I'm afraid I showed myself up by spitting it out. But the young Germans didn't mind. They took it all in good part and everyone had a good laugh. Strange to relate, but I have many happy memories of that time.

In any case within a few weeks almost everything was back to normal and there were hardly any German soldiers left in our village. The evacuated people had returned to their homes in the south of the country as the war moved on to France, where the Germans soon captured the so-called impregnable Maginot Line.

No one in Luxembourg could believe it, but worse was to come. Soon afterwards Paris fell, resistance collapsed and France surrendered. Few Luxembourgers had expected the French army to be defeated by the Germans – let alone so easily and so quickly. France had been our one abiding hope. Now it had fallen. The sense of shock and despair could be felt everywhere.

The Germans on the other hand were cock-a-hoop. Filled with pride and joy, they crowed over their great victory. They felt sure that England would be the next to fall to their unstoppable military machine. Over the radio they bragged loudly about their coming victory over the English and the ultimate triumph of the German empire. But they had overlooked one small obstacle . . . Winston Churchill!

In the meantime in Luxembourg, in the absence of our legitimate government, we had no choice but to look on helplessly as Hitler appointed the high-ranking Nazi Gustav Simon as leader of our nation, a man widely hated throughout the length and breadth of the land. In the name of Adolf Hitler, he soon set about changing our laws and issuing the first official decrees. We felt crushed.

On top of that the Germans were paranoiac in their determination to wipe out every trace of French from our national culture. In September 1940, when the schools finally opened again, all teaching of the French language was forbidden. German manuals propagating the Nazi creed replaced our former text books and all French-sounding names had to be changed.

For example, I became Emilia instead of Emilie and my brother Marcel became Marzellus, while all Marguerites became Gretchens. Even the French beret was banned. Anyone caught wearing it would have been very foolish indeed.

In the city of Luxembourg itself we suffered a further shock, in fact almost a desecration, when the statue of liberty, our 'Golden Lady,' as we fondly called her, was brutally knocked down. What's more we were forbidden to sing national songs like the 'Feierwon,' the 'Fire Engine' (our second national anthem, containing the popular chorus line 'We want to stay what we are; we don't want to become Prussians'), 'Zwee Kinnekskanner' (two Royal children), 'Lëtzebuerg de Lëtzebuerger' (Luxembourg of Luxembourgers) and our national anthem 'Heemecht' (Our Homeland).

The Luxembourg franc was replaced by the German mark and the civic rights we enjoyed as a free independent nation were abolished at a stroke. The Nazis had become the rulers in our country, our masters, answerable to no one but themselves.

On a lesser scale we had to endure the hardship of food rationing and the bureaucratic imposition of food tickets. But it would be idle to complain about this measure because it did ensure that food was distributed more evenly and fairly and that no Luxembourger actually died of starvation during the war.

Naturally we had to tighten our belts, as did every other nation under German occupation, not forgetting, of course, the British under the U-boat blockade of their Atlantic lifeline. We had to be satisfied with tiny quantities of meat, butter, flour, sugar, grease, soap, coffee, rice, tobacco and cigarettes, the quality of which continually deteriorated as the war went on.

Many goods disappeared in place of substitute or 'ersatz' food (a word that was soon to form part of the English wartime vocabulary as well), with roasted corn beans standing in for real coffee, rape oil for olive oil and saccharine for sugar, etc.

There were also many different artificially colored jams and honeys disguised under a host of attractive names and of course the ubiquitous black army bread known as 'Kamess,' which many people claimed gave them stomach ulcers. As for oranges and bananas, as well as all other exotic fruits, we even forgot what they looked like. They were to be found nowhere on the market.

For Christmas we got a 'special treat' from Eupen in Belgium of a small square of chocolate, which was in fact no more than an ersatz casing of artificially colored cream filling, barely recognizable against the real thing.

Clothes of every sort, fabrics and shoes were all a rarity too and could be bought only on the issue of a special written permit, which, as can be imagined, was far from easy to obtain.

Those of us who used to be choosy about what we ate and wore before the war soon learnt to be less fussy, but we never for one moment tamely submitted to any of the restrictions the Nazis imposed on us and cheated our occupiers on every possible occasion.

03 MUM AND DAD TAKE A BIG RISK

THE RAIN WAS BUCKETING DOWN and a storm howling all round the house and up and down the valley. It was a night to remember, that awful November evening in 1940 – and not just for the weather.

We had barely finished our supper and were still seated round the table, feeling grateful for the protection of a nice warm house, when suddenly there was a frantic knocking at the front door.

'My God!' cried mum. 'There's somebody out there.' 'It's the storm,' dad replied. Then came a second knock. 'Come in!' cried mum and dad together. But nobody entered.

Dad got up and cautiously approached the door. He opened it and looked outside. Still nobody. So he stepped out and disappeared into the rain and darkness. We waited for a moment, then mum got up to look out of the window and we followed. We stared out into the darkness but could see nothing.

Suddenly the door slammed. We all jumped in alarm, daring neither to move nor breathe. We knew someone must be out there.

The next moment the door swung open and in walked dad, accompanied by two men who looked like burglars or murderers. We were really scared, but they just seemed embarrassed. They were unshaven, poorly dressed and wet through. Strangely enough, they wore German jackboots and had German military caps on their heads. Who on earth were they?

My brother hid behind mum, who, in her nervousness, knocked over her coffee cup and spilt the contents all over the table. Dad soon calmed us down.

He explained that the men were French and had escaped from a German prisoner of war camp. They were now making their way back to France by following the railway track under the protection of darkness. My God, I thought – what a dangerous venture! But what were they doing in our home?

One of them pointed at the bread on the table and said in a hesitating voice: 'Un morceau de pain, s'il vous plaît. Nous avons faim' (A slice of bread, please. We're starving). Mum and dad understood as they'd learned French at school. I did too, because I had learned some before the war broke out. Then mum offered them a chair, but they refused. They didn't want to lose any more time.

Drawing: Silvio Marques

Dad quickly cut 10 slices of bread and mum buttered them. Unfortunately we had no more homemade cheese left in the dish and only the shells of cooked eggs remained amidst the disorder of the table. In a rush, dad opened the kitchen cupboard, grabbed a sausage and cut off a whole heap of thin slices.

In the meantime mum had quickly cleared the table and poured out a mug of coffee for each of them. Once more she offered a chair. This time they accepted and sat down gratefully. Without talking they wolfed down the bread and sausages and gulped down the coffee.

Mum then broke half a dozen eggs in the large pan and, five minutes later, the poor half-starved boys, were tucking into succulent fried eggs and emptying the coffee pot. 'Merci, merci, Madame' (Thank you, thank you, Madame), they kept saying.

One of them looked at my brother and me and said: 'I'm a father. I have three children at home.' He was obviously moved. Nobody said a word. Dad just looked sad, and mum wiped away a tear.

The two Frenchmen didn't stay any longer. Time was precious. But just as they were about to leave, one of them pointed to the shabby boots given to him by 'Les Boches' (as the French contemptuously referred to the Germans). Dad motioned them to wait and disappeared into the locker under the staircase from where he soon emerged with an armful of shoes of every imaginable type.

The Frenchmen couldn't believe their eyes. They didn't lose a moment trying them on, not caring how they looked but each choosing the first sturdy and reliable pair they could find. Then mum noticed their torn and soaked socks. She rushed upstairs and soon returned with two pairs of good woolen knitted socks.

In a moment, wearing dry shoes and socks, they were ready to leave. Then dad noticed their German caps. He snatched them off and threw them into the glowing fire of the kitchen stove, handing the boys his ordinary caps from the coat hanger. Mum wrapped up the rest of the bread loaf and sausage in a paper bag and stuffed it into their musette bag.

Gratefully they seized dad's and mum's hands, then swiftly turned to go. 'Watch out!' dad called out, as he switched out the light and opened the door. The two French soldiers rapidly disappeared into the darkness . . . and the storm.

Dad carefully shut and locked the door and switched on the light. We all stood around the table, with the wind howling in the chimney and the German military caps still burning in the kitchen stove. Nobody said a word. Then mum shook her head and broke the silence.

'Those poor boys! It's a long way back to France. Let's hope the Germans don't catch them – or they're dead.'

That was the signal for us children to open up and start bombarding our parents with questions. They gave a few guarded replies, but warned us to keep our mouths shut and say nothing to a living soul. Certainly not to any of the other children – or the Germans would throw mum and dad into prison.

That frightened us to death. We swore that we wouldn't. We were terrified at the thought of losing our parents.

The kitchen clock pointed to 7.30, time for us children to go to bed. But disturbed by all the excitement, we couldn't get to sleep. Mum knew that and stayed with us to pray for the two Frenchmen. Where were they now, we wondered at, surely at Roodt, the next village, or even further away in Menster? The storm was shaking the blinds, adding fuel to my anxious thoughts. It was a long night. But not as long as it just must have been for our two poor Frenchmen.

That what happened this night, stayed with us for a long time. We were continually being reminded of it by the many trains roaring past our house on the way to Germany, full of French prisoners packed in like cattle. They all looked like our two Frenchmen, miserable and desperate.

We wanted so much to wave to them, but we didn't dare, as they were guarded by grim-looking German soldiers with rifles. We wondered how many of those unhappy young men would ever see France again. In the days and weeks that followed I still remember the disappointment I felt because no more escaping French prisoners came along the railway tracks and called at our house on the way back home.

04 THE PRETTY DRESS THAT UPSET THE PRIEST

ON A LOVELY DAY IN MAY in 1941, I was standing outside the house with my mother, brother and duty railway-man John Bach when we noticed a large piece of orange-colored paper or cloth lying in the middle of the railway track some hundred meters from the house. What on earth could it be? We were puzzled. So my brother shot off to find out.

We watched him gather it up and hurry back, dropping it at my mother's feet. It turned out to be a mass of pure silk cloth. John Bach thought it was a parachute, but mom thought otherwise and laid it out in front of us. It was a beautiful long dress.

We stared open-mouthed. I thought it was a wedding dress, but mom decided it was a lovely ball gown, because it had neither sleeves nor collar, but a real square neck trimmed with a wonderful rose made of the same material. Mom fingered the expensive cloth and confirmed it was a taffeta dress that must have belonged to a lady with the waist of a wasp. When she lifted it up, to find out more about it, we noticed that its long stylish back was stained with black oil from the railway bolts. What a shame! Then she discovered a little French brand label inside the collar, telling us where it had come from.

That made sense, because a train packed tight with war booty plundered from France and on the way to Germany had passed by the house a quarter of an hour earlier. All sorts of merchandise, loot from castles and prosperous mansions, wine barrels and cases full of champagne-bottles, filled the wagons up to the roof. German soldiers kept watch by the doors to make sure all those stolen goods reached Germany safely. So our beautiful new gown, intended to make some German Fraulein happy, had flown out of a half-open door as the train sped by and fallen into our hands. But what could we do with it?

According to regulations, we were obliged to surrender the dress to the Nazi mayor at Roodt/Syr, but there was fat chance of our doing that! We would rather have burned it in the stove. So we decided to keep our mouths shut and hide it. Mom picked it up and bustled off into the house. Why not? John Bach agreed and we knew he wouldn't say a word.

That same evening mom took the dress to our friends the Giwers. Anny, a professional dress-maker, immediately spoke of 'haute couture' and couldn't stop caressing the moiré taffeta and admiring the style. Such a dream of a dress, she said, could have come only from a rich family, castle owners, the nobilities themselves. She couldn't resist trying it on and left the room with it only to return a little later looking like a princess. For a moment we were stupefied. She kept on looking in the mirror and preening herself as though the dress had been intended as a gift for her.

Then mom broke the spell and asked her if she could make a Sunday dress from this beautiful robe for Milly. For Anny was my skilled dressmaker and had kitted me out well from the scarcity of material available during the war. Mom was convinced that Anny could make a masterpiece for me out of that lovely gown.

Anny didn't respond right away. She continued admiring herself and was clearly reluctant to take off the dress. At last she seemed to accept the situation and disappeared to change back into her own clothes. She returned with the dress over her arm and quickly started taking down the measures she needed, noting them in her dressmaker's notebook. Although the dress was made up of tiny wedge-shaped pieces, which complicated the job she had to do, she managed to work it all out and by the time we left she was fully immersed in her task.

Around Pentecost I was called for the first fitting. I couldn't believe it when I saw myself in the mirror. I wasn't at all sure I liked what I saw displayed in that pink-orange material. But the dress was not yet fully styled and my ordinary shoes didn't match at all.

Some days later I came back for my second fitting, wearing my Sunday patterned shoes on this occasion. That was a perfect match for the outfit, which had also undergone a dramatic change. The dress now had a lovely collar and ruches, which could be tied back with a pretty sash. The whole effect was really quite fetching. Anny said she had had to use all her imagination in creating a pretty pattern out of that complicated ball gown. Well, she had certainly done a marvelous job.

But when she added short puff sleeves I became alarmed. I could imagine how our priest would react when he saw me wearing it in church. His ideas of how women should dress in church were rigidly old fashioned and he would brook no argument about it. However, when I mentioned my fears to Anny she said it was a risk we would have to take, because long sleeves would ruin the style and in any case there wasn't enough material left.

Back home I discussed my fears with mom and she had a talk with Anny. They decided that a small white jacket would throw the priest off the scent, but unfortunately I didn't have any such garment and didn't have a hope of borrowing or buying one in those grim days of austerity. Finally, we decided to take a chance and hope the priest would look the other way just for once. But my hopes were not high. I was already in his bad books for wearing sports socks. I was being thrown to the wolves and I knew it.

On Pentecost Saturday my dress was ready. Mom came with me to pick it up. I tried it on once more. It was perfect. Anny was satisfied, and felt proud of her work. She was entitled to. Mom and I felt really good about my having such a pretty dress at a time when any sort of clothes and fabric had become very scarce.

We knew of course that the dress would give rise to endless gossip among the village population, especially the families of the neighboring children and my classmates. So we carefully thought out the answers we would give to those nosy questions. One thing we knew for sure – we were not going to tell the truth.

On Pentecost Sunday the weather was ideal to wear the new dress. On the one hand I felt proud to be wearing the dress while on the other I was scared out of my wits. The service had not yet begun as I entered the church and our priest was still walking up and down the aisles casting an eagle eye over the congregation.

As soon as he saw me he raised his finger. It was the dreaded sign I knew only too well. It meant I had to leave the church. But I couldn't move. I felt as though I was glued to the floor. So he came up to me, pulled my puff sleeves, turned me roughly around and told me harshly that I had to dress more decently for church.

My worst fears had been realized. I was being publicly humiliated for wearing my beautiful new dress. I felt tears welling up in my eyes as I left the church, only too painfully aware of the other worshippers looking at me as I hurried out. Behind a neighboring farm I ran home beside the railway line.

'You see, I told you what would happen,' I sobbed to my mother when I got home. She just shook her head in disbelief. Then, practical as ever, she went off to fetch one of her jackets to put over my dress, but it didn't match at all. I continued to weep at the frustration and futility of it all, and did not return to Mass that Sunday. A narrow-minded priest had driven me out of church and made me very unhappy.

Meanwhile one of our neighbors called Sophie dropped by and mom told her what had happened. Sophie took me home with her and gave me a pair of long white gloves she had once worn with a wedding dress and which stretched right up to my shoulders. They completely hid my bare arms but the fingers were far too long and the whole effect was very odd. I looked like a praying mantis.

We all had a good laugh when I went to vespers in my new outfit. I got another nasty look from the priest, but there was nothing he could do about it. From then on, each time I wore my new dress for church, I covered my arms in those silly praying mantis gloves. They looked awful but did the job they were meant to do – get me past the priest's eagle-eyed inspection every time I went to church. That dress lasted two more summers, through times of dire shortage, when getting hold of clothing material was like discovering gold. I shall never forget it.

As for the priest, a year later he had the misfortune to upset one of our German schoolteachers and ended up in Dachau concentration camp, where he must have lived through a lot of much more shocking sights than the bare arm of a young girl.

05 HARD TIMES

LIVING UNDER GERMAN OCCUPATION during the war was indeed hard, but Luxembourgers couldn't complain about being short of money. We had plenty of German Deutschmarks, but there was very little to spend it on, and anything worth buying was soon snapped up.

On top of that was rationing. Ration tickets were issued each month and the German authorities kept us on a very strict quota. The weekly ration per person was 500 grams of black army bread, 100 grams of white bread, 200 grams of meat, 125 grams of butter, sugar, flour, pasta and coffee substitute. For bread weighing 1 kilogram, for instance, we had to hand over two tickets of 500 grams.

The shopkeepers had endless trouble using those tiny tickets. They had to glue them in their accounts books and check them against their supplies.

For housewives, who could barely run a household on those subsistence rations, the entire system was a nightmare. It was as much as they could do to squeeze one decent meal a day out of that miserable allowance.

It was easier in the rural areas, in the villages, where everyone had land or a garden of their own in which they grew potatoes and vegetables of every kind.

Necessity is the mother of invention, says the 16th century proverb, and our mothers proved it. Like magicians producing white rabbits out of empty hats, they dreamed up all sorts of meals concocted out of the food they were able to grow themselves. Our mother, for example, often used to give us thick vegetable broth with dumplings, 'omelettes,' pancakes and waffles. Heaven only knows how she did it.

Meat, however, was another matter. You could forget about meat on the menu every day, especially in the summer months, when fresh meat was a rarity at any time. No household possessed a refrigerator in those days, so during the hot days we had to be satisfied with dried meat such as bacon, smoked pigs' jaws and pork-necks.

Like all the other children, we didn't like this dried meat at all, so we had to put up with soft-boiled eggs and puddings instead. Like it or lump it was the choice at that time. The only exception was ham, which we couldn't get enough of, and mum was always watching to make sure we got no more than our fair share.

Another rarity was chicken, which was served only at the village fair dinner, known as the kermesse, but you could count on the good old rabbit always being on the Sunday menu. The Germans didn't take rabbits into account in their ration system so almost every family kept them as a stock food. Eventually, however, we had rabbit coming out of our ears and became sick of the smell of it, even though our mothers tried to disguise the taste under thick layers of sauce.

Sauce in fact was used widely to make up for the lack of variety in our meals, as well as serving as a substitute for fat, which, like bacon, lard and butter, had almost disappeared from the daily menu. The Germans called it 'Tunke,' their euphemism for fat substitute, because they didn't want to openly admit we were living on a skeleton diet under their occupation.

This shortage of fat meant that we hardly ever had French fries, which we loved. Instead we had to put up with boiled or steamed potatoes, made more palatable with a coffee fatty dip. Well, it was wartime, so we just gulped them down and made the best of a bad job. But whatever we did, potatoes remained the main course.

A supper dish served up everywhere was potatoes roasted with bacon, which made them crusty and tasty, accompanied by curdled milk. Awful as it may sound, it was better than black bread and coffee substitute, the only other choice available.

It would be expected that this crude diet would have made us all big and fat, but it didn't turn out that way at all. In fact, during the war years, most people were in better condition than they had ever been before, because that basic food was all we did eat, and only for the main meals. No sweets or treats or anything else in between.

Even the men, some of whom looked like bears before the war, walked around looking like weasels. At the inns and cafés all they got to drink was watery beer, as alcohol too was rationed. Nevertheless, even in the darkest days, the occasional illegal glass of wine magically appeared from under the counter to warm the cockles of a grateful Luxembourg heart.

As for us children, we had to make do with water, milk and an awful saccharine lemonade.

Believe it or not, milk was rationed too – even in the countryside, where cows were munching away in almost every field. Farmers were obliged by law to deliver a certain quota of milk per cow per day to the cooperative dairies. Milk could not be sold on a private basis and only one distributor per village was allowed to deliver half a liter per person in the evenings, after the cows had been milked.

This was barely enough to go round for most people, especially for families with several children. We were lucky inasmuch as our neighbor, the miller's wife, looked after us and always gave us an extra jar of lovely fresh milk. Mum would then skim off the cream to make white cheese, saving the rest for curdled milk, which we enjoyed as a special treat for supper during the summer months.

But getting hold of that milk was another story. The miller and his wife had to make sure the Germans didn't find out about their black market activities. So we children had to pick up the milk surreptitiously, sneaking round to the mill after dark, when the daily German patrols had retired to barracks for the night.

Those patrols were a curse to the farmers. From time to time a German police-man would unexpectedly turn up at a farm to count the livestock and check the deliveries of wheat, barley, oats, peas, beans, potatoes, milk and eggs against the registers.

When they discovered irregularities it was bad news for the maverick farmer, who soon found himself on the black list with a lawsuit to follow. Sometimes entire farming families were deported to Germany and replaced by German farmers, who were given their farms as well as their property and belongings.

But Luxembourg farmers didn't make it easy for the Germans to know what was going on behind the scenes. Unregistered chickens were always running around in the meadows adjoining the farms and most farmers had a stock of wheat balls hidden somewhere in the attic or the barn to be ground when the coast was clear.

In addition a few brave souls bred pigs and calves for their own consumption, hidden away and slaughtered secretly during the autumn or winter. Indeed a whole book in itself could be written on 'secret slaughtering' and the black market in Luxembourg during the German occupation.

Suffice it to say that many farmers ran the risk of punishment if they were caught. In the worse cases they were sentenced to deportation to Germany, and even minor offences such as farmers living off their own livestock or bakers keeping their own bread meant the loss of ration coupons for an entire year. Not a pleasant prospect in those barren times.

Nevertheless, when they were baking their own bread at the Schouttesch farm, risky or not, I had to be there. I just couldn't resist the temptation of those delicious freshly baked loaves. It made up for all the sweets that had long ago disappeared from the shops.

At home my mother was always unsparing of herself in the trouble she took to make life a little easier for us in those harsh times. One day she excelled herself when she produced a pudding, a sweet porridge, with dried apple chips and baked plums. We were over the moon.

On Christmas she delighted us with homemade marzipan, caramel candies and gingerbread. For us children, that was her 'piece de resistance' of the year. On Sundays too from time to time she would bake apple pie or cake. Then we would forget all about the war. Happy times indeed, in spite of all.

As the war went on, food and goods became more and more scarce.The reserves slowly ran out, with soap, coffee, flour, tobacco, nails and leather, yarn and wool, shoes and clothing gradually disappearing from the shop shelves. I well remember how the shortages affected my own family. It wasn't much fun for my mother having to wash clothes with some sort of soap substitute.

As a result people started to barter among themselves, exchanging every sort of food and provision imaginable. For example, farmers would exchange sausages for spices so they could get hold of salt and pepper to pickle their hams.

Most bartering took place between people from the country and merchants from the city, who came secretly by foot, train or bicycle with soap and coffee, cloth and wool, underwear and shoes, and similar goods, which they traded for the food that was in such short supply in the urban areas.

What the farmers valued most from the exchange was the tobacco and cigarettes the merchants were able to provide. From our perspective today, when smoking is recognized as a danger to health and widely discouraged, it may seem strange, even perverse, for Luxembourgers to have been desperate for a smoke while short of food and other necessities. But in those stressful times, when nobody knew about the danger to health, smoking was almost everyone's favorite form of relaxation. Farmers would do anything for tobacco.

When they couldn't get any, many of them stuffed their pipes with wild herbs and dried-up weeds from the forests. Some of them even went so far as to pay extortionate prices for a special tobacco ration card.

In all this give-and-take between town and country, which made life reasonably bearable for many people, it wouldn't be fair to disregard the city people who weren't merchants and didn't have goods to offer in exchange. These unfortunate people often had little or nothing to eat and had to make do with discarded potatoes or leftover milk.

Hunger forces the wolf to leave the forest, so the old saying goes, and that's more or less what these people ended up doing. Only they went in the other direction. They trekked to the countryside in search of food, offering the farmers high prices for flour, eggs and butter. But even then they had a problem, for they only had Deutschmarks, and many farmers didn't trust the German currency and wouldn't accept it.

What the farmers did want, however, was help on the farms, where they were desperately short of labor. So a compromise was soon reached, with the men helping out in the fields during their free time and the city wives sewing and mending clothes in the farmers' houses.

But farmers didn't always ask for help in exchange for food. When they had callers who needed food for sick persons at home, they accepted any form of payment, even, in some very sad cases, entire suites of furniture and possessions of personal value, such as family heirlooms and works of art.

By and large, however, it all worked out pretty well, with many old acquaintanceships and friendships being renewed in this meeting of town and country, but sometimes racketeers turned up and tricked the farmers into giving them bags of food they claimed they needed for their families and then went away and resold them to the needy at inflated prices.

Then came the snobbish town ladies with money dropping out of their ears who went from farm to farm offering to buy a single egg at half a Deutschmark (far in excess of the normal price at that time) because they didn't want to admit they were little more than beggars or feel they owed anything, even gratitude, to the farmers, whom they considered beneath them.

Drawing: Pascal Reimen

Finally a word should be said about those brave boys who refused to serve in Hitler's army and hid away in the forests, barns and other places of concealment. They had to be fed too and a lot of equally brave people took tremendous risks making sure they were.

But it was a dangerous business, for German patrols were constantly on the lookout for people on illegal missions of any sort, especially those giving sustenance to the heroic young patriots. The occupying Nazi forces called them 'enemies of the Fatherland.' So Luxembourgers risking their lives to feed our young 'refuseniks' got up to all sorts of tricks to outwit the German patrols, driving by night along secret trails through the forests and across the fields. They knew only too well that if they got caught they were in serious trouble.

Even when they could give a convincing explanation for their suspicious activities, they lost the food or goods they were carrying and were heavily fined for being in possession of extra provisions or being involved in secret activities. If they couldn't explain themselves, they ended up in prison – or even worse.

I still remember the poor man who cycled past me down the street over our level crossing one hot Sunday afternoon, when the bag he was carrying slipped from his bike and fell on the railway line, splattering yellow blobs all over the rails. I was on the spot in a flash. 'Hey, Mum,' I joyfully cried out, 'come and see – it's a real pudding.'

The cyclist turned round as I shouted and came back to gaze sadly at the contents of the bag spreading all over the rails. 'Yes, you're right,' he said. 'It's a pudding and an 'omelette' as well. I've just ridden forty kilometers from Lorentzweiler to the Moselle and now I've lost everything. And it was for someone who really needed it too.'

So sad and so typical of the awful times we were passing through
. . . .

06 WHEN FASHION WAS OUT OF FASHION

IT WASN'T UNTIL THE GERMAN soldiers emptied the Luxembourg shops of everything they contained that the Luxembourg population came to realize for the first time that they would have to learn to do without many of the commodities of everyday life they had taken for granted up until then. It dawned on them with heavy hearts that many of the goods that had vanished from the shops, such as clothing, footwear, fabrics and similar materials, were not going to be replaced.

In the city of Luxembourg the many well known Jewish stores like Renomée, Maison Moderne, Bourse, Jenny Gruenstein, Rosenstiel and Gilly had been confiscated by the new Nazi Administration and no fresh supplies were being sent to any of the other stores. In fact many of them were to remain almost empty throughout the war.

As for fashion, that soon became a distant memory. It was difficult enough just getting hold of enough to wear. People found themselves having to wear oddments of clothing until they wore out and slowly the situation began to get even worse. Clothing children became a nightmare as they quickly outgrew their clothes and pretty soon parents had nothing to clothe them in.

But German organizational genius came along to save the day. Their organization known as the Civil Administration hit on the brilliant idea of issuing ration tickets for food and clothing, giving the impression they were doing something to solve the shortage when in fact they were doing nothing, for the clothes the tickets purchased were of the worst wartime 'ersatz' quality. Not a thread of wool was used in their manufacture. They were simply awful.

Much of this clothing looked fashionable but it was rubbish. Luxembourgers called it 'Prussian trash' or 'Prussian wind.' Another description, 'German dirt,' was perhaps nearer the truth as the material was made up entirely of plant fibers like nettles and potato plant.

However hard you tried, you just couldn't make a crease stay in a dress or coat or any other item of clothing. It soon pulled out of shape, became shiny and rough and hung on the unfortunate wearer like washing on a line. As soon as the material was washed it turned as hard as a board, shrank and became shapeless, making it impossible to wear shirts, suits, dresses and similar clothing any more.

Shoes were the same. Those made of canvas couldn't be worn in the rain. They looked pretty enough, being made of fabric material of many different colors, but they didn't last very long, even in good weather conditions.

Sandals made with wooden soles were little better. They were like medieval Dutch clogs. Despite the soles being cut twice to make them pliable, they were uncomfortable to walk in and the clip-clop noise they made still echoes in my ears. It sounded as though the wearer were riding a horse.

As for leather shoes, they could be obtained only on the black market. Later, during the winter months, the Germans issued special tickets enabling us to buy shoes of a rigid leather with rubber soles. Even then, special ticket or not, to actually get the stores to let you have a pair you had to have been a good client of theirs before the war. Otherwise it was back to the clogs and the clatter.

Nevertheless, Luxembourgers didn't go around in rags. Everybody made the best of the situation and helped out, trading and swapping with one another, buying and selling clothes on the black market, doing just about anything to get by.

From worn-out old clothes we made new clothes, while old dresses, coats and suits were cut up, washed in Panama wood, rinsed in vinegar, sometimes even dyed, and then turned inside-out. What was a coat would become a dress and that would in turn become a skirt.

Sometimes two different types of cloth were used for the top and bottom halves of dresses. If a dress was too tight, it would be widened by the use of light and dark matching strips, which sometimes even managed to start a new fashion or trend, while strips of fur and velvet were added to the bottom of coats to make them longer and prettier. There really seemed to be no end indeed to the sartorial ingenuity of the people in those times of privation.

Knitted-wool wear was very popular at the time. If you had some wool or were able to get hold of some on the black market you were sitting pretty. If not, all was not lost, for you would simply take something old apart, especially sweaters, cardigans, socks or pants, and knit something new.

In order to straighten out the old wool, it was first rolled around the top of a chair, then tied together in a couple of places so it wouldn't get mixed up, and then washed. That way you could get a nice smooth thread again. Most of the time the wool used consisted of two matching colored strands, which gave it more strength and made it look good as well.

Stripes and squares were by far away the most popular patterns. Flared dresses too were very much in demand in those hard times. Nevertheless, a dress was a dress and whoever could get hold of enough wool to knit one didn't have to worry about freezing to death in those bitterly cold wartime winters.

A large number of people raised sheep during the war, not only for the nice soft lamb's-wool but also for the meat, which, like that of rabbits and chickens, was not rationed.

As far as the wool was concerned, the only drawback was the awful chore of cleaning it. Sheep owners in our locality spent a lot of time doing that in the Knaeppjes's and Schouttesch's houses, where they prepared the rough wool by fluffing it up before spinning it into good thread for the production of warm sweaters.

Both sweaters and socks were patterned in the braided style so popular at the time and the socks were knitted in pink, blue, yellow or green cotton, which, amazing to relate, could be bought in the shops every now and then.

The women hardly had no time at all to themselves. They seemed to be forever preoccupied with mending holes in the clothes, sometimes one after the other, or stitching in patches to cover the holes where the material had simply worn out. It was of course to be expected with the poor-quality material the clothing was made of, but it didn't make life any easier for them.

Gloves, mittens, scarves, earmuffs and hats were knitted from all sorts of leftover wool. Some of them may have looked a little odd, even comical, I must say, and wouldn't have looked at all out of place in a circus with a red nose to accompany them, but they all caught the eye and were highly individualistic. We certainly demonstrated the truth of the old saying that necessity is the mother of invention.

For our family it was a blessing in disguise that my maternal grandmother, or our 'Ditty' as we called her, had passed away in February 1940, just before the Germans invaded in May. The new clothes we all wore for the funeral in Menster, where she had lived all her life, saw us comfortably through the war years.

The dark-blue coat with gold buttons kept me warm for a couple more winters and was not wasted when I grew too big for it because our clever dressmaker friend Anny Giwer was able to turn it into a cute little dress. The nice pleated skirt and jacket made from black and white hound's tooth served me well for many years first as a suit, then as a dress with a red and white bow on the collar and finally as a skirt.

Even my black lacquered shoes lasted the course. When they became too small, shoemaker Giwer chose the ingenious if somewhat Procrustean solution of cutting off the toes (the toes of the shoes not mine!) so that I could wear them for another precious year.

It wasn't so easy for my brother. You could search high and low but you would never find any men's clothes on the wartime market. So my father's clothes had to be adapted. From a pair of father's trousers, tailor Freylengesch Batty made a fine pair of boys' trousers and a suit, and from one of dad's coats he conjured up a rainproof jacket, similar to a duffle coat, for the bad weather. Our Marcel couldn't have been happier with his catching Sunday outfit.

But my parents had to switch their imagination into overdrive when Marcel needed a special suit for his first communion, a major rite of passage when children everywhere in Luxembourg are photographed in all their finery parading through the village and during the ceremony at the church. As usual, in Luxembourg at that time, my parents had to resort to the most popular means of exchange in wartime use – black market barter.

They had a calf secretly slaughtered at the mill and secretly sent the meat along with the flour to the underground resistance in the forest at Differdange. After a few days some top-quality dark-blue wool material appeared on the table at the mill and was soon transformed by Tin the tailor into two handsome suits to be worn on the big occasion by my brother and his friend Emil from the mill. The magic wand of barter had done the trick once again.

The rest was plain sailing. For Marcel's black lacquered shoes and silk armband, some chickens and geese had to make the ultimate sacrifice and my mother sent a rabbit, eggs and butter to Madame Nelly, the milliner from Luxembourg city, who duly presented her with a new black felt hat with a paradise bird on top. Just about everything in those days operated through the secret channels of barter.

Fashion in fact had never really had its day. It may have been suppressed but it still reigned supreme behind the scenes. We just made do and produced our own fashions. The reality of that could certainly be witnessed in the great splash of patriotic color that filled the streets on Liberation Day, when all the Luxembourg girls appeared in their red, white and blue outfits to rapturously welcome the triumphant American soldiers.

07 THE GESTAPO and NOAH'S ARK

I HAD NO IDEA of the shock in store for me as I left for school on that fateful day on 19th of June 1942. I knew there had been a lot of trouble between our local priest and our new teacher, Mr. Gierens, a German transferred to our school during the Easter holiday of 1942. They just didn't get on. But I never could have guessed what it would lead to.

Our former Luxembourgish teacher, a great friend of the notorious Luxembourgish collaborator and traitor Kratzenberg, had been promoted to a teaching post in Germany and shortly afterwards Mr. Gierens came from Germany to take his place. At first he seemed to be all right, and we would even have accepted him had he not been a Nazi. But it didn't take long for things to change.

Each day it began to become more and more apparent that he had been planted in Luxembourg for the principal purpose of indoctrinating the Luxembourg children in his charge. It was in fact his mission – unknown to us children of course. It was on the express orders of Gauleiter Gustav Simon, the official German-appointed leader of Luxembourg and Hitler's personal representative, that German teachers were appointed to posts in Luxembourg with specific instructions to change the minds of the young people of Luxembourg and inculcate a love of Germany.

Gierens was true to his mission. He never ceased to glorify the name of Adolf Hitler, his beloved 'Fuehrer,' or to try to whip up our enthusiasm for the new empire Hitler was planning to build in Europe. And not a day passed without a glowing report about the triumphs of the German Army, the Wehrmacht, as well as the hated ritual of the 'Heil Hitler' salute at the beginning and end of each class.

But we 'stupid Luxembourgers,' as Gierens called us, never seemed to be able to get our 'thick heads' round what our Nazi instructor was always ranting on about. He told us that Mendel's laws proved that the Germans were a superior race (Mendel proved nothing of the sort – he only demonstrated that hereditary characteristics are transmitted without change) and that one of history's greatest conquerors, Attila the Hun, known as the Whip of God, was a German, whereas he was in fact a Mongolian.

He also taught us that Frederick 1 or Barbarossa, who spent most of his life fighting against other Christian rulers all over Europe, was a humble king who submitted to the Pope at Canossa (which he did - but only after being defeated in battle at Legnano), and that Charles the Great (better known as Charlemagne) succeeded in uniting Germany and France only after a blood bath, which Gierens seemed to think was a great achievement.

Drawing: Laurinda Dos Santos

But such was our dislike of this arrogant strutting little Nazi that we didn't believe a word he said. He was wasting his time with us. We preferred to believe what our parents told us both about the Bible and the Germans.

But trouble really started when Gierens started to pull the Bible to pieces. He got a lot of fun mocking the story of Noah's Ark. He called it a 'load of nonsense' that the priests were trying to stuff into our heads. He laid it on pretty strong when he told us it was impossible to build a boat big enough to hold a pair of every kind of animal, to take care of them, feed them and then put up with the smell. Just one of the many 'lies' told to us, he claimed, during our religion classes.

We got sick to death of hearing him constantly repeat the military expression 'Jawohl' ('for sure'), which Nazi officers and other officials used all the time. But after a while it lost all meaning. It simply went in one ear and out the other.

As soon as the priest heard what Gierens was up to, he hit back in our next Sunday religion class at church by telling us how important the stories in the Bible were to us Catholics and what nonsense was being spread around by atheists, freemasons and other enemies of the Church. He was furious and didn't mince his words, making it perfectly clear to us what he thought of Gierens and his teaching.

Gierens exploded with anger when he heard what the priest had been saying. 'This black mole, this German hater, this agitator, has to be destroyed,' he screamed. The effect on us children can be imagined. We were frightened. Especially when Gierens started to interrogate us.

'What rot he preached in church yesterday! What did he mean by "rubbish"? Whom was he getting at?' Gierens of course knew perfectly well whom he was getting at – and so did we. When he questioned me, I replied: 'I don't know.' For that he called me a 'stupid goose' and scribbled something on a piece of paper.

Heaven only knows what it was.

All morning there was tension in the air. We were all so scared that no one moved. Gierens kept on calling us names such as 'rhinoceros,' 'hippopotamus' and similar stupid insults. We just kept quiet and didn't blink an eyelid.

Naturally we told our parents what had happened as soon as we got home. They were all worried and very soon the whole village knew about it. People had a bad feeling about the whole business and it was said that Gierens was not alone in his attack on the priest. There was a lot more behind it than met the eye. Little did we know how true that was. And what's more there was worse was to come.

On Friday morning the priest's housekeeper came to my mother and said: 'If Father Zeimes goes to jail, it will be the fault of the children. Someone ought to go to Roodt-Syr and tell the German police what Father Zeimes really said, because he's being accused of telling a lot of lies about Gierens and Hitler.'

I couldn't believe it with my own ears. It was nonsense and I said so to my mother in no uncertain terms. Nevertheless, she took me on an hour's walk to the police station, where I told the policeman on duty simply what had been said at school and at Sunday school.

Drawing: Joâo Gomes

I can still remember what a frightening experience it was. To an 11-year-old child the impressive-looking German policeman looked like a giant. Even though I had done nothing wrong, I felt afraid. But he just took notes and said he'd pass it on to whoever was in charge of the affair.

On our way back over the railroad track, we met Father Zeimes at the small railway level crossing. We wanted to tell him how it went at the police station but he told us he was being watched and couldn't talk to us. He said the Gestapo was in the village and probably waiting for him. He must have known what was going to happen ....

By the time we arrived home it was all over. In no time at all the news had spread through the village like a bush fire. We heard about it from the lady next door. 'The Gestapo searched Father Zeimes' house,' she said. 'Then they arrested him and took him away in their car.'

Even now I remember the shock as the words sunk in. Father Zeimes arrested and in jail! And it was our fault. For a moment I didn't react. Then I ran up to my room, threw myself on the bed and cried my heart out for ages. My mother tried to calm me down, but there was nothing she could do. I really felt it was on us children, including me, who were responsible. My world had collapsed. How often, I thought, had Father Zeimes told us that no good ever came from telling tales, especially about reverend people like priests — and here was I involved in such an affair. It was days before I could find any peace of mind.

The village was in a state of shock. Rumors were rife. We heard that Father Zeimes was already locked up in the Grund prison in Luxembourg City. We no longer had a priest and had to go to neighboring villages for Sunday mass. No more priest in our village! No more mass in our church! At that time it seemed to us in our small Luxembourg village as though the world was coming to an end.

Shortly after the arrest the Gestapo turned up at school. How disgusting they looked, I thought, in their black leather coats and boots, with their silly long green caps emblazoned with the German eagle. One of them carried a briefcase, which he opened conspicuously, almost gloatingly, in front of children almost paralysed by fear. You could almost hear the silence.

Then the inquisition started. They bombarded us with questions, obviously intending to intimidate us. We didn't give a single reply. We just sat there, frightened out of our wits and ashen faced, some of us unable to stop trembling.

Many of the questions were about the song 'Christ King,' which we sang in church with an arm straight out and two fingers pointing up like an oath. They accused us of making fun of the Hitler salute. Although most of us were subdued and tried to keep out of trouble when we answered their questions, a few of us finally had the courage to give the answers the Gestapo didn't want to hear.

But we also kept quiet after the Gestapo threatened to send us to Germany to be taught their way. What was the point of making a fuss? There was nothing we could do.

The Gestapo didn't leave it at that. They came back a couple of times to read out reports and plied us with question after question. By the time they had finished our heads were spinning and we were lost in the jungle of questions they had trapped us in. We just let them talk on and remained subdued. That was of course what they wanted.

At home and in the playground we spoke more freely among ourselves, of course, but even then we had to be careful, as there were spies among us. Trinn and Mia Busch, for example, from the German household, where Gierens was living.

On one occasion I couldn't keep my mouth shut and accused our two German school friends of denouncing Father Zeimes. 'Be careful,' Mia said, 'or you will be keeping him company.' I bit my tongue, but it was too late. The following day a letter arrived from the Nazi commune leader, a Luxembourger acting as a Nazi Ortsgruppenleiter (town mayor) and whom we mockingly referred to as the 'Gauleiter.' I was to go alone to Roodt-Syr to see him in his office, formerly the home of our Jewish baker, who had managed to escape into hiding somewhere.

By the time I arrived I was a jelly-bag of nerves. I was placed in a chair opposite the 'Gauleiter' and had to listen in obedient silence while the monster accused me of being a 'revolutionary and an enemy element.' I wasn't sure what that meant by 'element' but his face told me it wasn't good. I defended myself as best as I could, bearing in mind that I had to protect my family as much as myself.

The 'Gauleiter' disliked my parents intensely and was responsible for my father being sentenced twice to two years' hard labor on the German railways. What's more, he didn't like my relatives either, because they came from his own hometown, Mensdorf.

If I didn't improve my behavior, he barked, I would be sent to an 'education camp' in Germany. The words sent a chill right into my very bones. I got the message loud and clear. After that, like most other Luxembourgers, I kept my mouth shut in future.

At Olingen we heard little news of Father Zeimes. He appeared in court in November 1943 for the mere formality of a trial. The verdict was of course a foregone conclusion. A couple of my classmates were summonsed by the Gestapo to appear as witnesses, but they didn't ask me, probably because I already had the repute to be an 'enemy element' and they thought I would stick up for the priest and give them the answers they didn't want to hear.

As for the Noah's Ark quarrel, it didn't even feature among the countless hostile activities Father Zeimes was accused of. It was never more than a pretext in any case. He was of course found guilty and sentenced to 22 months' penal servitude the notorious Dachau concentration camp (Zuchthausstrafe), where he remained until he was liberated by American troops in April 1945.

Gierens, who didn't know what to do with the stupid Luxembourg 'mules' and knew he was hated by the entire village, didn't return after the summer break. But after the war he was captured by the Luxembourg secret service in the town of Hermeskeil, near Koblenz. Like so many ex-Nazis, he had gone into hiding and was hoping to escape identification.

He was interrogated in Trier and held there for trial and sentence. While in jail he wrote to Father Zeimes to confess his guilt and ask for mercy, but he claimed that he didn't betray the priest to the Nazis. He blamed the Busch family for that. He was in fact a talented artist and, in atonement for his sins, he promised he would paint two anti-war murals of 30 meters each for the church in Olingen if Father Zeimes would withdraw the accusations against him.

We had to wait a few more years before we learned the full story, which we did when Father Zeimes published his 'Manuscript.'

Did Father Zeimes forgive him? Of course he did. As a Catholic priest what else could he do. Christian charity called for nothing less. In fact Father Zeimes did far more. He withdrew his complaint. So the real traitor got away with it again.

08 A NASTY SHOCK FOR THE GERMANS

MY FATHER AND I HAD NO IDEA of the drama about to unfold when we cycled from Olingen to Munsbach one lovely Sunday afternoon in June 1942. But we had a somewhat sharp reminder that we were living in an occupied country with little control over our own destiny when we stopped at Neuhaeusgen, a region acclaimed for its cherries, to try to buy some of the juicy cherries we had seen in the roadside orchards.

The people there told us they were not for sale. The Germans had estimated the amount of fruit the orchard could produce and had ordered the bulk of it to be exported to Germany as soon as it was picked. What was left wouldn't even be enough for the local people. My father was upset, but by now we were getting used to this sort of treatment from the Nazis.

So we rode down through Oetrange to the Plaitrenger farm, where every morning my uncle Vic used to collect milk for delivery to the dairy and occasionally do some shopping for the farmer. Dad knew we would get privileged treatment there – and we did, coming away with our bicycle bags filled with cherries.

When we arrived home my mother was delighted with our success. After we had stuffed our bellies, she saved enough for several jars of canned cherries for the coming winter as goodies of every sort were scarce during the war.

It was that evening that we got the first inkling of trouble ahead. Father had been intending to go for a drink at the local café, but mum reminded him he was due to catch the early train to return to Germany in the morning, so he changed his plans. Little did we realize how fortunate that was.

While we were sitting outside the house on the bench near the door, railway-man Nick Houdrement from the nearby village of Menster - Uncle Lou to us children - came and joined us. He was working on the night shift and told us that the nine o'clock train had been derailed that morning at Manternach, where the last car had jumped the rails. No one was hurt as the carriage was empty.

We were relieved to hear that, but wondered how it could have happened. Uncle Lou talked about sabotage, but my parents doubted it. No one would dare move against the Germans at that time.

In any case it was bedtime for my brother and me, but it was a hot summer's night and, even with the windows wide open, we found it hard to sleep, because the adults stayed outside on the bench talking endlessly about the derailing at Manternach. I was still awake when my parents came up to bed, but eventually I drifted off.

Shortly after midnight a big bang woke us all up. What on earth was that ? Mum and dad jumped out of bed and rushed to the window, with my brother and me right behind them. They leaned out and talked to Uncle Lou swinging his carbide lantern down below. He called out that it must have been the freight train that had just passed. It hadn't long gone down into the valley known as the 'hog hole' when a great explosion made the rails vibrate.

A couple of minutes later the silence of the night was again shattered by the insistent ringing of the telephone in the railroad-crossing shack. Uncle Lou ran to the shack and took the call. Someone from the station at Wecker and Roodt was on the line asking what had happened to the train that should have passed through the station by then. They also heard the bang and wondered what it was.

What was worse was the news that another train, packed with soldiers on leave from the front line, was soon to arrive. Uncle Lou was ordered to check the track down to Betzdorf to see whether the train had passed through there. My father dressed quickly and took over Uncle Lou's duty for the time being. Mother made us go back to bed. Eventually Uncle Lou returned and I crept back quietly downstairs to hear what was going on.

He phoned the station at Wecker and Roodt and told them that the train had left the rails in the 'hog's hole' and was lying on its side by the track. Several carriages lay strewn alongside the track, twisted and entwined over broken rails, some on top of the others. The driver was in a state of shock and the guard, who had been thrown down the slope into the creek, was unconscious. It was a mess.

Drawing: Gloria Antunes

Poor uncle Lou didn't know what to do. He had done his duty and followed the guidelines all railway-men were given, but nobody knew what he should do next. The line from Luxembourg to Wasserbillig was immediately closed to all further rail traffic and a general alert was called along the entire line. The phone too fell quiet. Everywhere the slogan was: 'Maul halten – Feind hoert mit!' ('Keep your mouth shut – the walls have ears!.')

Father remained in the shack with Uncle Lou while my mother and I went back to bed, but none of us was able to sleep. In the morning we found ourselves in the thick of it. Two German policemen on motorcycles roared into the village and stopped at our house. They interrogated Uncle Lou alone in the shack, telling my father to stay in the house.

Mother came to our room and told us we should pray for father. He could well end up in jail. My God! Was it going to be a repeat of what happened 10 days ago when they arrested the priest? I still hadn't got over the shock of his arrest. I was frightened out of my wits.

The Germans then came into the house and cross-examined my father in the kitchen. He had to tell them exactly what he had done and where he had been on Sunday evening. They took note of every little thing. They eventually left to put several of our neighbors through the same ordeal.

When they'd gone I came downstairs and joined my parents in the kitchen. My mother said: 'Thank God you stayed home last night, Dad.' My father didn't reply. He just poured himself a strong shot of schnapps.

A little later a Gestapo man with a dog approached from the direction of Betzdorf. The dog was following a scent trail and went straight towards Uncle Lou and jumped up at him. The poor man was terrified and could only just about manage to stutter out why the dog had targeted him. He carried the scent the dog was following, he explained, because he had followed the railway line all the way of the accident area. The Gestapo man seemed satisfied, ordered the dog to calm down and left. Uncle Lou ran straight to the toilet.

News of the derailment spread like a bushfire through Olingen and the nearby villages and it wasn't long before crowds were soon flocking to the scene of the accident. But the police were tough and turned them back in no uncertain manner.

Soon the road from Olingen to Betzdorf and the neighboring country roads were swarming with Wehrmacht soldiers. The 'hog's hole' was closed off and ringed by German troops. Farmers were not allowed to work in their fields and the schools were closed.

The Syr creek, the forest, the hedges and even the sewerage system were checked by the SS and their dogs. Two soldiers kept close watch over our house and everyone was afraid to go outside. It was like a curfew, and the worse was yet to come.

Around noon German soldiers surrounded Olingen. The village, which was already in the Germans' bad books because the priest had been thrown into jail by the Nazi police barely two weeks before, was then invaded. Every house, barn, stable and shack was searched. Every screwdriver and every pair of pliers (the tools used to dismantle the rails in the 'hog's hole') was held to the noses of the SS dogs. Joseph Buerg's blacksmith's was turned upside down.

One of the local young men, Ziirden Emil, fell under suspicion for no other reason than having shaved off the long beard he usually had that very Sunday. Another villager, Paiffesch Jull, a friend of Ziirden Emil's, counted himself the luckiest man in the world and couldn't thank Emil enough. He had wanted to go and pick cherries in the 'hog's hole' on Sunday but Emil had reminded him that the trees there hadn't grown any cherries that summer. An even closer shave than Ziirden Emil's!

The next to be interrogated by the Germans was the farmer's leader, known as the 'Ortsbauernfuehrer.' He had to face some pretty tough questioning, but he gave nothing away. Schoolteacher Gierens took the German side as usual and denounced the perpetrators of the derailment for bringing trouble on the village. But nobody took any notice of him. We all knew what he was.

While the search for the guilty party was still going on, the furious Germans went full speed ahead with the repair work. A building team arrived with a giant crane, but had a lot of problems at first using it effectively as many of the coaches lay on their side jammed between the Ziirdemount cliffs of the narrow gorge there. Nevertheless, they worked hard day and night and managed to clear half the track for the passage of rail traffic within a day and a half.

In the meantime a bus took passengers between the section still under repair, Roodt to Betzdorf, and two days later the 'wheels were once again rolling for victory' ('Raeder rollen fuer den Sieg'), claimed the Nazi propaganda channels broadcasting one of their well-known slogans.

But the Germans were still enraged by their loss of face. In newspapers and on large posters they advertised a 100 000 Reichsmark reward (big money in those days) for information leading to the arrest of the saboteur. Their inquiries and investigations dragged on for weeks.

On the 8th of September, when Catholics celebrate the birth of the Virgin Mary, they conducted a house-to-house search of Olingen, but came up with nothing. I can still see the Germans in our kitchen threatening to confiscate my mother's coffee set, though goodness knows what that had to do with finding the man they were seeking. Frankly, it was little more than looting.

In September the Germans started mass deportation to Germany of all Luxembourgers suspected of anti-German activities anywhere in the country. It was not in fact specifically connected with the derailment in Olingen, though that is not how people in the village saw it at the time, including my own family.

Everyone became scared, but no one from Olingen or our locality was taken away. We owed our good fortune to the abovementioned 'Ortsbauernfuehrer,' who stood up for the village under close Nazi interrogation and defended us against all accusations of implication in the act of sabotage. Unfortunately, no one spoke up for him after the war when he was thrown into jail.

The saboteur was never caught by the Germans. It was not until some years after the war, when he received an award from Prince Félix, that we discovered he had been a member of the Luxembourg Resistance from Grevenmacher. His courage may well have been heroic at that stage of the war, when the Germans seemed to be well on their way to final victory, but his heroism was at the expense of a guiltless village of some 200 people whose lives he had put in extreme danger. He was not considered a hero in Olingen.

09 TALE OF A TINY CHURCH

THE BELLS OF A FASCINATING little Luxembourg church rang out for the last time in 1978. It got taken over by a larger modern church needed for the increasing population of the Syr valley. Fortunately the tiny church of Roodt, where I used to attend mass as a child in 1942 and 1943, still stands today, properly preserved as a reminder of the 18th century. Today it is used for concerts and art exhibitions.

As I grew up, I often admired the old church on my way to the neighboring town of Mensdorf, where I used to go to visit my grandparents. With its low narrow door, little windows and large cross under a small roof, it was tiny in comparison with the larger church in Olingen, but it had a charm all of its own.

What made it special for me, however, was the tall narrow tower, so much more attractive than the short stocky tower of the church in my home village of Olingen. As a child I used to think that all churches should be like the old Roodt church, with long high towers, reaching up to God like hands in prayer and seen by everyone from far and wide.

I first started going to church at Roodt in 1942, shortly after the Gestapo had arrested our priest and left our own church at Olingen with no one to celebrate mass. First of all we went to the neighboring villages of Betzdorf, Flaxweiler and Roudemer for Sunday school and mass, but the Roodt priest, Father Felten, wanted us to attend mass at Roodt as he had been delegated to stand in for our former priest.

That didn't please us children of Olingen at all. We didn't get on with the children from Roodt, who called us 'cheeseheads' because, so they said, we were just 'peasants.' Quite understandably, we didn't think too much of them either and called them 'tinheads,' as they were the children of tradesmen and industrial employees, most of whom were horribly snobbish and looked down on us 'country bumpkins.'

We had also heard that some people in Roodt didn't go to church at all, which was unthinkable in those days in rural Luxembourg, especially to our young unworldly minds. In fact our own priest had already warned us about Roodt's iniquitous ways before his arrest and our family hairdresser confirmed it. We readily believed him because he used to shave the Roodt priest's tonsure and was in a position to know. We really didn't like the idea of having to go to mass at Roodt.

Oddly enough Father Felten seemed quite happy with the people of Roodt, despite all the stories we had heard about poor mass attendance. As for Father Felten himself, we already knew a little about him. He often used to attend funerals in our parish church and say mass on our Virgin Mary altar. At first we rather liked him. Whenever we met him in the street, he would raise his big Roman hat in response to our usual greeting: 'Blessed be Jesus Christ.' Then he'd say a friendly word or two before walking off.

But all that changed in 1942, when he became parish administrator and started riding his bike to Olingen to teach us children the catechism. He didn't make our Bible lessons as interesting as Father Zeimes had and he made us learn everything by heart. He was very strict too. If we failed to pay attention and learn our studies, he would bawl us out and frighten us to death. What's more, he insisted that all of us, our parents as well, went to mass at Roodt. This upset a lot of people, as everyone thought the Roodt church was far too small to hold us all.

The local Roodt people too looked quite taken aback when they saw us for the first time, streaming in through the small door of the bell-tower and up the aisles of the tiny church. Nevertheless, we all somehow managed to squeeze in. In fact it wasn't until we reached the children's places that we met a problem, when we found that the local children didn't intend to let us in. But Father Felten wasted no time putting a stop to that, quickly coming down to make sure we all found a place.

First of all we found it hard going. We had not been used to kneeling on such low benches, with nowhere to hold on to, sitting like cats on a hot tin roof, but had to make the best of a bad job and get used to it.

For me it was the perfect opportunity to study the church from the inside. 'Quaint' is the word that springs to mind and that's what it was. The ceiling was low and vaulted, the great thick walls painted with flowers and the altar was carved out of wood and decorated in gold. It was quite dark inside too, so different from our own large well-lit church, although the Roodt candlelight was so much brighter.

The passage to the altar was so narrow that when the priest approached with the three altar boys they just about managed it. Later, during the 'Asperges me' ceremony, when the priest passed by in his long choir gown, held up by the altar boys, to bless us with holy water, I felt I'd had a shower rather than a blessing. My friends Martha and Marceli and I got a sudden attack of the giggles but were 'miraculously' cured when we caught the fearful eye of the priest.

'Introibo ad altare dei' rang through the church and everyone made the sign of the cross. The organ burst into tune, the few members of the choir raised their voices in a hymn of praise and the altar boys cried: 'Mea culpa, mea maxima culpa.' To our surprise we could hear it all, loud and clear. In our church, where we had to sit farther away, we always had to strain to catch the words.

Before the sermon, Father Felten removed his robe in front of the Virgin Mary altar next to us and then slowly ascended the steps to the pulpit. To our amusement the wooden steps made an awful creaking noise, a distraction that would never have been tolerated in our church.

But we dared not let the priest see we were amused as we had seen what had happened to some of the boys who had started to show off and play around. The priest wasted no time in coming down and sorting them out. You didn't fool around with Father Felten. Unless of course you were a fool!

As the mass continued, Bruck Corneille, one of the altar boys, began to swing the incense pot to and fro, quickly filling the church with incense smoke. I loved the fragrance, but poor little Nathalie, a friend of mine, went quite pale and had to sit down. Half way through the mass, the church resonated to the sound of a sweet little bell, attached to a rope in the bell-tower.

For Holy Communion we had to worm our way out of the small packed benches and then struggle back again, which was even more difficult. And after the service our knees really hurt. But we soon forgot about our pains as we filed out past the holy-water receptacle and noticed the teacher standing there and looking very angry. As the boys came by we saw him pick one of them out and give him a good slap for misbehaving during the sermon. What a different world in those days!

Drawing: Viviane Deutsch

As we came out of the church we shyly eased our way through a large crowd of people standing around and talking together, reading the notice boards or simply enjoying each other's company. Some even went off to pray over the graves of the loved ones they had lost. Such a crowd! And at Roodt .. ? Obviously the stories we heard about the Roodt people not going to church were just a lot of unkind gossip.

The atmosphere became even better as we walked home. We passed my dressmaker, Miss Uselding, who returned my friendly nod with a nice smile, while her hat slipped across her head and her bag slid off her shoulder. We tried hard not to show our amusement and embarrass the poor lady but it all helped us to feel more relaxed and better about everything. Then we really began to feel at home as we passed many other people we knew, such as the priest's housekeeper and a friend of my mother's called Keup Anna.

As we approached our own village and began to find ourselves on familiar ground we soon regained all our old confidence and began to get a bit bawdy, talking and shouting loudly as children tend to do the world over. One of the boys started mocking the Roodt teacher while another cracked jokes about our former teacher. It was all nothing more than good harmless fun, but we agreed it would be better not to talk about it to the other children or we could have got into trouble.

We still argued of course that our own church in Olingen was larger and more beautiful than the Roodt church but had to admit that we were wasting our time thinking about it as our priest was in jail and masses were no longer celebrated there.

Gradually we got used to our new place of worship and even began to develop affectation for it. Then one day we realized what a truly lovely atmosphere reigned inside that little church and how really nice and friendly the people of Roodt were, turning out to be very good Christians indeed, despite all the rumors to the contrary we had heard.

It all seemed like the mist had lifted, like a revelation, almost a small wonder fulfilled by the old little church of Roodt, during the wartime.

10 WHEN PIGS KEPT US NICE AND CLEAN

TODAY WE TAKE SOAP FOR GRANTED, spoiled as we are for choice by all the exotic sweet-smelling varieties in the shops, but during the war toilet soap was a luxury we could only dream about, like so much else we look upon as essential to the good life these days. The only soap available to us during the grim years of German occupation was 'Rifsoap,' a ghastly gray-green product which had a tendency to skin you alive and had a smell that would have killed a vampire at six paces.

Our clothing didn't fare much better either as the only washing powder on the market would have made a better paint stripper. Its acidic qualities meant that any housewife who used it ran the risk of destroying the clothes she was washing.

But, as usual when times are hard, people found ways to help themselves and many housewives produced their own soap, including my mother, who kept us clean with her own secret formula, the key ingredient of which was the grease from a pig. The complete recipe, which was boiled in an old metal washing basin my mother had had for years, was made up as follows:

eight pounds of pig's grease;
two pounds of soapstone;
a fifth of a liter of linseed oil,
six liters of water ;
a final dash of pine sap.

The whole concoction was boiled in mother's old metal washing basin until the soapstone had dissolved, when eight more liters of water were added. The muddy looking mixture had to be constantly stirred and kept on the boil for one and a half hours. The brownish water that had collected at the bottom of the pot was then emptied away, leaving just a greasy top layer. A further eight liters of water and a pound of salt were added and the mixture slowly brought to the boil. Then, last of all and to give the soap its sickly sweet smell of incense, my mother would add the pine sap that we children had gathered from the pine trees in the nearby forest.

The yellowish mixture was finally poured into a mould to cool. When it had solidified it was removed and cut into about 20 pieces, which lasted my mother for a whole year. Mother was naturally proud of her handiwork and it was, I must say, a pretty good soap, especially for those times of shortage and deprivation.

In fact we had more than just a good soap to thank my mother for, because during the war many Luxembourg housewives used nitrophenil, which was later found to be a carcinogenic agent.

Then in the winter of 1942-43 our soap supply came under threat. Mother's beloved old washing basin sprang a leak - just two weeks before she was due to make next year's provision. The need to get it mended in good time was urgent and I got the job of taking it to the next village, Junglinster, to get it repaired. I had no excuse as we attended school only in the mornings during the German occupation. I didn't mind. In fact I quite looked forward to it.

But Junglinster was seven kilometers away and I had no idea of what was in store for me. I shall never forget that awful journey. These days, whenever I drive along that road in my car, all the thoughts and feelings I had as a child come flooding back to me.

Off I set in good heart, confident I could cover the distance there and back in no time at all. When you're 12 the world is your oyster and is out there just waiting to be conquered. I was boosted by the thought of the reward mother had promised me. She said she would buy me the poetry album I had wanted for a long time. In my little mind it was just going to be a nice little outing.

It was a cold but clear sunny January afternoon. The washing basin was strongly tied onto my sledge and I marched eagerly onwards. Downtown in one of the biggest farmhouses in Olingen, they were threshing the grain; in another, belonging to friends of the family, they were making schnapps, the wonderful smell of which reminded me of plums.

Oddly enough even the slight pong of manure that rose from the farms I was passing didn't strike me as being at all unpleasant. I felt the same about the half-frozen yellow-brown liquid manure trickling along the open roadside gutters, all part of the romance of winter in my farming village.

The roads were covered in snow, which had sand and ashes sprinkled all over them outside the farms. As I passed the last house in my village, I noticed that the water supply had been completely frozen. Neighbors were helping to thaw out the main supply pipe by building a big fire above it at the side of the road.

Once outside the village, however, the street began to be very slippery. From there I could see my schoolmates shooting down a hill on their sledges and toboggans. I longed to join them, but the thought of my reward kept me plodding on.

In Roudemer, where the whole village seemed to be deep in a winter sleep, the only sound to be heard came from the blacksmith's, where a horse was being shod. The road began to rise and became more slippery, making it difficult for me to keep my feet, especially as I had nails in the soles of my shoes. If I walked in the side I sank in the snow up to my knees and if I stayed on the road I kept slipping over.

Not a soul was to be seen, not a car on the road. The abandoned old Weimesch mansion up on a distant hill looked eerily frightening, almost ghostly, and the silence began to close in. Suddenly I felt very lonely and more than a little afraid, as gloomy thoughts began to fill my mind.

I wondered what my father was doing at that moment in Germany, forced to work on the railways in the Saar River area and living in a railway carriage in the bitter cold of that winter. I thought too of our priest, held prisoner somewhere in a concentration camp.

Drawing: Joâo Gomes

Then my thoughts turned to Stalingrad, where the Germans claimed they had won a great victory. I knew otherwise. On the

English radio we heard quite a different story, which was broadcast all over Luxembourg and filled us all with fear for our poor Luxembourg boys forced to fight in that icy hell against their will. Many of them fell there and those who returned - many of them terribly injured or mutilated - were never the same again. Even those who returned after the war with their minds and bodies intact could never forget the horror they had lived through.

Fiels Joss, the son of one of our local farmers, had lost a leg and two other village boys, Welter Jempi and Scharels Joss, were never heard of again. I remembered also Pitze Pol as having been deported with the Luxembourg "Volonteer – Company" to Weimar (Germany). All over the country the story was the same. My God, I wondered, when is this terrible war going to end.

Then I thought of our Grand-Duchess Charlotte in exile in England. When would she return? A few days earlier on her birthday, the 23rd of January, her son Prince Jean, addressing the Luxembourg nation on the English radio, had lifted our hearts with a message of hope for us all. That cheered me up and I continued on my way in a happier frame of mind.

Then my thoughts were suddenly interrupted as I tugged too hard on the rope of the sledge and landed on my back. I scrambled back on my feet only to tumble again before I reached the crossing at the Gonderange signpost, where the small train known as 'Charly' came hissing and whistling past me in the sharp cold air.

Finally the commercial town of Junglinster came into view, lifting my spirits as I struggled to keep my feet on the icy roads. What a contrast after the silent slippery roads of the slowly darkening countryside! The town itself was a hive of activity, with the saws of the great timber yard, Clement, squeaking away and huge piles of wood lying all over the yard.

I suddenly felt alive and happy again in the hustle and bustle of Junglinster after that cold and lonely journey. At the hardware shop, Mr. Beaume, the ironmonger, inspected the basin and shook his head. 'It won't be easy to mend,' he said, 'but I'll have to do it as you won't get a new one these days.' He said it would be ready in a week.

Relieved I decided to relax and look around the shop, where I saw some good carving knives, which were difficult to get hold of in wartime Luxembourg. I wanted to buy two, but Mrs. Beaume said I could only have one. I pleaded with her, as I knew how happy it would make my mother, who had been trying to cut with a blunt old knife since rationing had come into force. Eventually Mrs. Beaume gave way and let me have them. I danced happily out of the shop.

Now I was faced with the sobering prospect of the journey home. It was already past four o'clock, the sun was disappearing behind the hill and it was getting very cold. The snow crunched under my feet, my breath turned to smoke and my feet into blocks of ice. But once I reached the Gonderange signpost I felt the worst part was over. Now, I thought, it's downhill all the way, and I could use the sledge myself, as it's no longer needed to carry the washing basin.

But as soon as I sat on the sledge I was in trouble. It took off like the wind and within seconds was completely out of control. I panicked and tried to brake with my feet only to send the sledge spinning like a top until it tipped over and took me with it into a ditch. After I had clambered out, I was afraid to sit on the sledge again, but I had no choice. The road was covered in ice and I couldn't even stand up on it let alone walk home pulling the sledge.

But this time I eased on the foot brake from the start, keeping the sledge under control until we reached Roudemer, where the streets were not quite as treacherous. By then night was falling fast and I was really looking forward to getting home. My ear lobes tingled, my nose ran and my fingers hurt with cold even though I wore mittens. I glided safely the rest of the way, singing the popular Afrika Corps song of Lilli Marlene. Goodness knows why. I certainly had no love for the German Army but singing the universally popular song did manage to keep my spirits up.

It was pitch-black by the time I reached Olingen. All the blinds were drawn in the houses in compliance with the German blackout regulations, and the only lights relieving the darkness came from the blue bulbs in the stables, where the animals were being fed. The streets were empty and no one could be seen, but the smell of black sausage filled the air and I suddenly felt very hungry.

At last I reached home, where dinner was on the table – jacket potatoes, leek creamy dip and baked apples. My favorite! Mother was happy that I was back, and I was in heaven. When I unwrapped the knives she hugged and kissed me. While I was eating I talked and talked with my cheeks glowing red with the welcoming heat. Then all of a sudden I could no longer keep my eyes open. I was asleep as soon as my head hit the pillow and slept blissfully right through a long, long night just like a baby.

Two days later I got my reward. I took the train to Luxembourg City and bought my poetry album. The following week, on a cold gray day, I was back on the road to Junglinster to pick up the basin. But the streets were not so icy this time and in any case I was better prepared. I was wearing socks over my shoes, a muff for my hands and a thick scarf round my ears and neck. Some of the people I met on the way must have thought I was a Russian!

But the trek proved to be worthwhile when I got to Junglinster. The basin was ready at Beaume's and I managed to run a few errands for my family and friends at the same time. I bought some soapstone for my mother at the chemist's and some medicine for a neighbor's granny. The only disappointment was the carving knives. I wanted to buy one for the 'godmother' at the mill, who was always so kind to us children and to all the neighborhood, but they were out of stock.

On the way back, with a job well done, I was in a happy frame of mind and dreaming about the delicious caramel candy my mother was cooking for me. But I wasn't so happy about the sledge. I couldn't sit on it any more – the basin had got my seat! I just had to pull it all the lonely and laborious way.

None of that mattered though when at long last I reached home and caught the intoxicating smell of caramel candy drifting from the kitchen. For a Luxembourg child in those grim war years, caramel candy was a very special treat and made those long journeys to Junglinster all worthwhile.

11 A SECRET KILLING

IT WAS EARLY IN FEBRUARY in the harsh winter of 1943, my father was at home on a few days leave from his railway job in Germany – and he was up to no good. Well, at least in the eyes of the Germans, for if they knew what he was about to do he would have been in serious trouble.

It was the time of year to kill a pig, which of itself would have attracted no interest on the part of the Germans as long as it was declared at the animal count. But my father had planned to kill two – one to declare through the usual channels and the other to keep for our own needs without informing the authorities.

It was early in the morning and everyone was jittery. Quite naturally ! If he and the friend who was helping him were to be betrayed by someone or caught red-handed, the least they could have expected under the Nazis for killing a pig without reporting it would have been prison or deportation. It was a risky business.

My father was up early. It was still dark when he went into the laundry room at the back of the house, started a fire in the oven and placed a large basin of water on top, adding coal to bring the water to the boil. In the kitchen too a fire was already roaring away in the stove and two big pots of water on top were starting to boil.

My mother was also up and about and got my brother and me up earlier than usual. She wanted us out of the way before the slaughtering began. When we came down the stairs into the kitchen we noticed the water in the pots boiling in big waves and the windows all steamed up. It was as warm as on a baking day. Mother poured out some water into two small basins for us to wash in and we really enjoyed it in such a warm and cozy room.

But mother wasn't at all happy. The pig that was going to be secretly slaughtered was going to be cleaned out in her spotlessly clean laundry room - and she didn't like the idea. As a house-proud lady she knew what a terrible mess it would create and she knew she would be left to clean it up.

She was dashing between the house and the washing house, fetching pots and two big potato baskets lined with towels, anxious to get the nasty job ahead over and done with as soon as possible. Once my brother and I had dressed she gave us a breakfast of bowls of cubes of bread, sugar, milk and coffee known in Luxembourgish as a 'braech,' which is not as awful as it sounds. We were still spooning it up when the 'executioner' walked in.

We knew him very well as Knaeppjes Leo. He was a great joker and a typical village character, but I am afraid I found him deeply repulsive. His big fat red cheeks were glowing like beacons and his round nose was dripping. Ugh! Ready for the slaughter, with his high green boots, blue apron over his big bulging belly and a sack under his arm, he certainly looked the part for the job he was about to do. And not only looked . . . he made our kitchen stink like a stable.

Then my father came in and immediately filled three Karely glasses (little glasses used for schnapps) with schnapps and told me to go and get his workmate Uncle Lou from the railroad shack. It was Uncle Lou's spell of duty that morning, which was why they had chosen that day for the killing. He was a good friend, he knew what was going on and could be trusted to keep his mouth shut.

The three men lifted their glasses and gulped down the contents in one go. My father refilled the glasses. Then the railway bell rang to signal the arrival of the train. One last hurried drink and they were ready to go and do their grisly job.

Uncle Lou went to close the gate over the level crossing. Leo took the knives out of the sack, pulled up his shirtsleeves and tucked in his long undershirt. My father put on mom's old apron, grabbed a lantern and a pot and ran with Leo into the pigsty.

The pigs were killed the very moment the train to Betzdorf screamed by with a thunderous roar. It was timed to perfection. No one heard a sound from our house because the noise of the train muffled the dying screams of our poor dear pigs.

My mother, who had ran after the men into the pigsty, returned with a pot brimming with blood. She kept stirring it quickly so it wouldn't clot and then she poured it into the earth pots. I closed my eyes tight. The sight sickened me.

My brother was so upset he ran crying from the house, but my father swiftly and strictly brought him back before helping Leo lift the officially slaughtered pig on to the bench in front of the pigsty. The other one, our 'black' pig, was loaded on to a wheelbarrow and hidden away in the laundry room.

Outside it was neither dark nor light and no one was around except of course Uncle Lou. Thank God, we were safe. Even now I still remember the sense of relief I felt then as a child.

My brother and I watched from the kitchen window while the men got down in earnest to the awful business of cleaning the pig on the bench. Father went into the kitchen and poured the boiling water from the pots on the stove into the buckets and carried them out to the slaughter bench, where he poured the steaming water over the pig.

Leo used a special knife to scrape off the pig's hair, which fell to the ground with the water to form a river of brown slush in the snow that wended its way to the gutter. Father called mom and asked for the basket with the towels. Then Leo, in one slash, cut open the pig's belly. A cascade of lungs and liver, and just about everything else, fell into the basket. Blood leaked into the snow and turned to ice.

Father carried the basket back into the washing house while Leo busied himself cutting off the pig's head. I could have cried. I felt so sorry for our lovely pig.

Shortly afterwards we left for school, the scenes of the 'massacre' still fresh in our tender young minds. But when we came running home at midday, the sight of our pig's carcass hanging on a hook from the rung of a ladder, frozen stiff, with the head hanging on another rung behind, hardly troubled us at all. By then we had forgotten how upset we had been by the spectacle of the slaughter and we started to amuse ourselves counting the ribs, which we knew gave the juiciest pork chops.

Drawing: Filipe Da Costa

The other pig, the one we were hiding from the Germans, was hanging on another ladder in the laundry room. Father was still washing the floor and cleaning the basin, frantically shoveling and clearing away the bloodstained snow. After he had got rid of every last trace of blood, he closed the windows and locked the door.

Then a lovely rich smell of cooking drifted in from the kitchen and any remaining thoughts of the sad fate of our pigs were finally banished from our minds. Mother had fixed the lungs and the liver. What a feast we had! It was even better than the town fair dinner we used to enjoy so much.

But the afternoon was another story. Then came the horrible job of cleaning and gutting the pig, a messy job that was left of course to mom, who made soap from the guts and black pudding sausages was filled in the thin intestines.

It was stressful too as much of the work had to be done undercover in case anyone found out what we were up to. My poor mother was flapping about like a bird in a cage, frantic to finish her work before the arrival of the 'politically correct' weighing master from Roodt. She was anxious to ensure that nothing was left around to arouse the suspicions of an official whose first duty was to his German employers.

At around four in the afternoon Knaeppjes Leo came to help my father take our pig down off the ladder. They carried it into the kitchen, where Leo took his big knife and a saw and cut the pig into four. Then came the difficult part of his job.

He skillfully and selectively cut off chops here and there to remove enough of the pig to give the impression that the pig we had slaughtered for the animal count was a complete pig but simply a short one. The chops we kept were a 'hidden extra,' not recorded and kept out of sight of the authorities, thereby ensuring we got more tickets for our meat ration..

My father and Knaeppjes Leo certainly didn't suffer from a bad conscience on account of the trick they were playing on the Germans. Their only concern was to make sure they weren't caught. After all, every Luxembourger with any spirit was out to cheat the Germans if they could get away with it. It was more than a national pastime. It was a badge of honor.

So brazen in fact was Leo in his un-repentance that he carried on practicing one of his tricks by tinkling around with our scales. But that time he almost came a nasty cropper and got us all into serious trouble, as you will discover in the next chapter.

12 CAUGHT RED-HANDED ON THE FIDDLE

NIGHT HAD FALLEN and it was dark outside. Father had closed the shutters and blacked the windows out from the inside, as the Germans had ordered. The scale was ready in our kitchen. Right next to it lay a pig's head and one of the pigs cut in quarters. To help ease the tension, father was helping mother process the remains of the lard through the grinder. The weighing master from Roodt hadn't arrived yet and father was getting restless. He had good reason to be.

Then suddenly, as the seven o'clock train thundered by, the kitchen door opened and in came the man they were waiting for, Mr. Birebam. His job was to weigh the slaughtered animals, note their weight and pass on the information to the German food office, where the weights were registered. This office would then issue meat tickets according to the weights of the meat submitted, with fewer tickets being given for animals weighing a lot and more tickets for animals weighing less. It didn't pay to register too much meat. If you did, you could end up with no meat tickets for months on end, sometimes even up to a year. We all ended up playing a sort of game, trying to trick the weighing master.

That day Mr. Birebam was moaning about the number of people in the parish that had slaughtered their animals, giving him too much work to do. We were the last on his list and all he wanted to do was to get on with the job and go home. So without further ado he took his papers from his bag, put his glasses on and got down to business.

My father placed the first quarter on the scale. Mr. Birebam peered over his glasses, counted the kilos and noted the weight. And so it went on until all four quarters had been weighed. The front quarters weighed about 18 kilos and the hind 20 kilos. The man from Roodt shook his head. He couldn't understand why the pig wasn't heavier with those lovely big hinds. He looked at my father suspiciously and asked him to weigh the head.

Father was taken aback and tried to take Mr. Birebam's mind off the pig's head, explaining that the head was only meant for aspic anyway and wasn't worth the trouble. But the weighing master became suspicious and insisted on the head being weighed. Father added the weights in a hurry: one, two, three kilos, but nothing happened, not even a flicker of the needle. Then, almost in a panic, he added another kilo, which made it four, far too much anyway for a pig's head, but still the scale didn't register. The head weighed nothing!

'What the devil is the meaning of this?' screamed Mr. Birebam. Father, clearly rattled, started again, even more hurriedly than before, but with no more luck.

The weighing master slowly removed his glasses and looked straight at my father: 'You're cheating, aren't you?'

Father looked as though he wished the earth would open up and swallow him and must have been cursing Leo Knaeppjes, whose idea this whole fix was. He was so nervous he was making it worse for himself. Mr. Birebam ignored him and started putting the weights on the scale himself. One, two, three kilos and again the needle didn't move. 'There is something wrong with this scale,' snapped Mr. Birebam, picking it up angrily and shaking it. Then he removed the head and turned it upside-down. 'Just as I thought,' he muttered.

Drawing: Silvio Marques

Then he lifted it up and showed us the little weight he had found attached with a string to the lever on the bottom of the scale. Father stood there open-mouthed and speechless. Mother stopped ironing and went red in the face. Our tongues were tied. No one could put the blame on Leo Knaeppjes, whose great idea it was to put the string there. We had been caught red-handed and that's all there was to it.

After the initial shock, father tried to play the incident down by laughing it off, offering Mr. Birebam a glass of Quetsch schnapps. But the officious weighing master wasn't going to let us off the hook so lightly. He grimly insisted that the pig be weighed again.

The weight on the bottom was removed and the scale brought back into balance. But now each quarter weighed up to three kilos more than before, and the pig's head tipped the scales at about seven kilos. Mr. Birebam, satisfied with a good night's work, accounted for every last gram and made sure we knew how lucky we were that he wasn't going to report us to the food office for trying to defraud the authorities. We were lucky to have escaped with only one black eye.

As Mr. Birebam carefully put his glasses away and his books and papers in his briefcase, my mother came in from the living room and handed him a handful of cigars. This was a diplomatic masterstroke at a time when cigars were worth their weight in gold. His big eyes beamed and his face cracked into a rare smile. After that my father even managed to persuade him to empty the schnapps. Then, just before he left the house, the cockles of his heart suitably warmed by mother's inspired gift and father's schnapps, he told us he was going to be generous and deduct some of our kilos. How lucky we were! Not only did we get away with it, but we came away smelling of roses!

Shortly after Birebam had left, Leo came over to cut up the pig or, to be precise, two pigs. Again, as was usual in those days, out came the schnapps and my mother bustled off to make some coffee. Then dad told Leo what had happened. He burst out laughing, his big belly shaking as he slapped his knees. Well, by that time we'd got over the shock and had begun to realize how lucky we had been, so we soon joined in the laughter too.

It turned out to be quite a celebration. Mother served the coffee, real coffee, smelling as it did before the war, and father poured a plum schnapps into Leo's cup, which made it smell as coffee used to at the town fair after Sunday lunch. It soon loosened Leo's tongue and he told us exactly what had happened last year when the weighing master had arrived at their place.

They had also been trying to beat the system, killing two pigs, one officially and the other secretly. During the afternoon, prior to Birebam's visit, he and his brother Jemp had been distilling schnapps and, true to form, had ended up drunk. When Birebam arrived, they rushed out to bring in the official pig. His brother grabbed the first half and carried it through the barn out to the scale in the covered yard. Leo followed with the other half. When both halves were lying side by side, Mr. Birebam shouted out: 'What's this then? A pig with two tails!'

In a flash of a second, the two brothers sobered up, stared at their handiwork and then started blaming each other. Jemp gave Leo a piece of his mind and Leo lost his temper and attacked Jemp. Birebam promptly jumped in and tore them apart, giving them such a tongue-lashing that the noise echoed up and down the entire street and even set all the dogs off barking. Marie came rushing out of the house and put her hands over her head in disbelief when she saw the 'pig with two tails.'

The upshot was of course that they had to submit the other two halves, cursing while they were doing so. But there was nothing they could do about it. They had got what they asked for. That same evening Marie, also as a gift offering in reparation, walked all the way to Roodt with a basket filled with eggs, butter and sausages for the Birebams. Again diplomacy paid off. Only one pig was registered in their name at the food office. We all fell about laughing when he told us this hilarious story.

Then the work started in our house. Leo sharpened his knives while mother took everything off the table and cleaned it up. Father and Leo carried the secretly slaughtered pig into the kitchen from the washing house and lay it on the table. Then, with no more room in the kitchen and the grisly work about to begin, my brother and I were sent off to our beds. But we couldn't fall asleep with all the talking and laughter in the kitchen going on late into the night.

The next day my father pickled the meat while mother cooked the pork chops and made some pâté. Well, all's well that ends well, and that particular episode in the harsh years of Nazi occupation ended very well indeed.

13 THE BBC AND OLINGEN MILL

DURING THE WAR when bread was rationed and became rare, especially white bread, Olingen Mill got a new lease of life. Every day farmers from the region came with their horses and wagons and brought their wheat to be milled and their oats and barley to be coarsely ground.

The miller was great fun, a natural joker, but he was no fool – he knew his business. His customers liked him, because he gave them good service and sometimes did a little black market milling on the side for them too.

For us neighborhood children the mill was a place that drew us like a magnet. There was the old lock that diverted the water from the Syr and the Roudemer creek to the deep water of the pond that turned the turbine of the mill. I well remember how this dark and dangerous water both fascinated and terrified me.

During heavy rainfall or a thunderstorm the miller had to keep a careful eye on the lock. Nevertheless, it sometimes flooded and left the mill stranded in the water like an island.

There was so much to see and do there. In winter, when everything was frozen solid, almost all the village children went on the pond to ice-skate with or without skates. On hot summer days the big boys had the perfect place to swim while the little ones had a great time teasing the fish with their toes.

Everyone liked the miller, whom we called 'Uncle Joss.' He was usually covered in white dust and always as mischievous as a monkey. He loved children and often let us play hide and seek in the mill. I still wonder who had the most fun when he pulled us up with the sacks of grain, dipped our heads in the flour, shoveled grain on us to cover us up, or put us upside-down in an empty sack.

With the miller's wife, my brother, Marcel, and I felt at home. We were the playmates of their adopted nephew, Emil. We called her 'Godmother' and we could get anything we wanted from her.

Many were the times she baked us pies, cakes or cookies or something else we liked. What's more she was very good at cooking, and with good reason. She had been a cook at Ansembourg castle before she met and married Uncle Joss, who had been the driver of the count who owned the castle.

I always loved the stories she told us about the castle and count and countess, who owned it. They talked a lot in French, especially when we children, with our 'big ears,' were not supposed to be listening. It made no difference either when the Germans forbade the use of the French language. That did not stop the miller's wife, for she and Uncle Joss were actively interested in politics and had strong opinions of their own.

Before they married and took over the mill, they had traveled a lot with the count and countess all over Belgium and France and had spent most of their free time reading countless magazines, papers and books. As a consequence they were both very well read.

In their living-room hung a big map. The countries which had been occupied by the Germans were deliberately painted red by the miller's wife. She marked Rommel's moves in North Africa with white drawing pins and Hitler's battles elsewhere with pins connected by blue wool. I was often present when she explained the moves on the map to the farmers in the mill room.

But what really amused everyone was the way she was fooling the Germans by marking out the map in the colors of the Luxembourg flag, red, white and blue, which were forbidden by the Germans. It was the secret little joke enjoyed by all the Luxembourgers who called at the mill.

She always kept up with the latest news and knew just what was happening at any time in the battle zones. Apart from reading the newspapers, she had her radio, which took pride of place in the built-in closet in their living-room or 'stuff,' as we called it (and still do, even today), and brought the news of the German Army's daily report (the 'Wehrmachts-Bericht'), as well as the ranting and raving of Hitler's speeches, straight into the house.

But the German propaganda didn't fool the miller and his wife. In fact the miller often made fun of the Nazi lies. For they knew different. They had access to the BBC, which at that time Luxembourgers called 'The English,' and, in the company of people they could trust, they were only too eager to explain what the BBC had reported.

Many people didn't have a radio at home in those days, while others who had small children or nosy neighbors didn't dare listen to a foreign channel. It was strictly forbidden by the Nazis and if you were caught you quickly ended up in jail. So a lot of Luxembourgers were only too happy to hear news from 'The English.'

For them 'The English' was the voice of the Free World – and the voice of hope and liberation. It was the only way to find out what was really happening on the war front.

The V for Victory signal, taken from the opening chord of Beethoven's Fifth Symphony and corresponding to the letter V in the Morse code (three short beeps and a longer continuous signal), became a symbol of hope throughout German-occupied Europe. It was also the very same sign made famous throughout the world by Winston Churchill, a sign both of victory and a two-fingered salute to Adolf Hitler.

On Sunday mornings at nine o'clock the English station broadcast a special Luxembourg program. The speaker on those occasions was the Grand-Duchess Charlotte herself, her husband Prince Félix, Prince Jean or a member of the exiled Government.

It was the only way they could keep in touch with their people, and for the Luxembourg people it was a holy hour. It was what they all longed for - the ray of hope they needed to keep faith with themselves, a light in the darkness heralding the coming of the liberating Allied forces. And the clarion cry 'Haalt hinnen den Bass, dir gitt de Preisen erëm lass!' ('Hold out against them, you will get rid of the Prussians again!') was heard throughout the land and inspired fresh hope and courage wherever it rang out.

Naturally not all Luxembourgers managed to hold their tongues and some gave way and provoked the Germans, who were not slow to retaliate at the cost of many a Luxembourg life.

The Germans of course were enraged by these broadcasts. They tried to jam the station by every means at their disposal and sometimes succeeded in making it impossible to understand what was being said. Even worse, they managed to cut off the electricity at nine o'clock for an hour, and this really upset the Luxembourgers.

It was at such times that the miller came into his own, proud that it was he who owned the mill and was thus able to provide the power needed for the broadcasts his countrymen looked forward to so much. But the miller's wife could not contain her excitement and told all her clients what was happening. Word soon got round and by and by more and more people came to the mill to hear the latest news.

It became noticeable how many people from the Minette, the industrial south of the country, came and went by the mill. Was it for news, to barter, to buy . . . or something else? It was in any case obvious that something was going on down at the mill.

It was also no secret that BBC broadcasts were being listened to there regularly every night. Some of the people who had their noses in everything were permanent visitors.

On the few occasions my father managed to get home for a weekend from Germany, where - like many Luxembourgers known to be anti-Nazi - he had been sent to do forced labor on the railways for the German war machine, people came to he mill to hear his news of what it was like in Germany as well as listen to the BBC. They were anxious to know what the German people really thought about the war.

I really didn't like it when my mother and father went to the mill at night. At those times I just couldn't sleep. My imagination tormented me with horrible visions of prison, concentration camps and deportation. I was terrified the Germans were going to raid the place and catch them all listening to the BBC.

Well, it continued like this for a while until one Sunday two members of the Gestapo did in fact arrive to do a random check. Emil, thank God, saw them coming and warned the miller just in time.

When they searched the place they found nothing amiss. The radio was tuned to the Berlin station, the mill was running normally, with Molly the dog barking frantically, 'Lili Marlene' the cow mooing and the turkeys and geese gobbling and screaming as though the Christmas axe was about to descend on their silly heads. Nevertheless, the two Gestapo looked everywhere, but they couldn't find anything wrong and finally gave up – to everyone's tremendous relief.

Uncle Joss now understood why Taerens Pir, the farmer's leader, had warned him to be more careful. Pir was a native German who had married an Olingen girl many years ago and settled down on her farm as a farmer. He was good guy and had protected the people of Olingen on more than one occasion.

After the Gestapo visit the evenings round the mill had to stop. News from the miller's wife's dried up and she became upset if anyone tried to ask questions. Clearly she was shocked by what had happened and didn't trust anyone any more. She even refused to let Emil play with us. We found that difficult to understand.

But it wasn't only at the mill that the mood had changed. Everywhere in the country people grew depressed by the endless wait and the Nazis, seeming to sense their coming defeat, started to treat Luxembourgers more and more brutally. Some people lost hope altogether. The promised help failed to arrive and the Luxembourg ministers in exile, speaking from London, sometimes talked nonsense and made us very angry.

Drawing: João Figueira

110

For example, on one occasion one of our ministers said that any Luxembourger who joined the German Union (the 'Volksdeutsche Bewegung') would be held responsible after the war. We really didn't need that. It only went to prove they had no idea what it really was like for the ordinary people living under the jackboot of the Nazis in Luxembourg. Everyone was upset by this lack of understanding.

'It's easy for them to talk,' people grumbled, 'safe and cozy in London while we're in the shit up to our necks in Luxembourg.' Those broadcasts should never have been made. They had a bad effect on local morale and succeeded only in confusing the people of Luxembourg.

Then on the morning of the 6th of June 1944 everything suddenly and dramatically changed. The Germans announced that British and American forces had landed in France. We couldn't believe it. The BBC hadn't said a word about it.

When our Prime Minister, Pierre Dupong, addressed us at noon on the radio from his London exile, he confirmed the wonderful news of the invasion and advised all Luxembourgers to remain calm. The news spread like a bush fire. Everywhere Luxembourgers felt a great sense of relief. Many listened to 'the English' all afternoon, some even covering their radios and their heads with a blanket.

At the mill in Olingen they rejoiced, but remained cautious. They were still shocked by the Gestapo visit. They were right to be careful, for there were still some bad times ahead. The Germans were more aggressive than ever and didn't hesitate to kill or imprison at the slightest provocation.

But when the hour of liberation finally came, one handsome young man personified the joy of Luxembourg when he stood openly and happily at the door of the mill. We didn't know him, but he knew us. All of us – and by name. How come?

Well, his name was Josy Puetz from Oberanven. He had been drafted as a conscript into the German army, like so many other young Luxembourgers, and had not returned to his unit after home leave. He had been hiding in the mill ever since.

We couldn't believe it. And to think he'd been hiding there when the Gestapo searched the place! How did the miller and his wife manage that? Well, read on. . . .

14 THE SECRET OF OLINGEN MILL

ON THE EVENING of the 15th of February 1944, a young Luxembourger set out from Oberanven to walk under cover of darkness through the neighboring villages of Niederanven and Roodt to his final destination at the mill of Olingen. His father followed later by bike. They both prayed they wouldn't be noticed. If the German police, who were always on patrol somewhere or the other, had an inkling of what was really going on, they would have been in serious trouble.

During the day the young man had said goodbye to his friends and neighbors. His month's leave from the German army was due to end the following day, when he was supposed to travel to Regensburg in Germany to be checked in at the barracks in the evening. Then he was due to be sent to the Russian front for the second time, but had sworn that the devil himself wouldn't get him there. It was time for Josy Puetz to desert.

One plan had already failed, when a boy from Kautenbach tried to smuggle Josy over the border into Belgium but had been caught by the Germans. Then, in desperation, Josy's father tried to get someone in the family to hide his son, but the first two relatives he approached refused, quite understandably, because to do so risked imprisonment or even death.

Then he tried his distant cousin, the miller of Olingen, and his prayers were answered. The brave miller and his wife didn't hesitate for a moment, agreeing at once to hide Josy in the mill.

As soon as Josy and his father reached the mill, the miller wasted no time, showing Josy his room right away. He was to share it with nine-year-old Emil, the miller's nephew, who was already asleep and didn't hear a thing. Otherwise it was business as usual at the mill. The miller's wife was milking the cows while her brother, Tin, was getting ready to catch the train to Germany the next day to visit Luxembourgers deported by the Nazis.

So Josy's father didn't stay long. He rode home quickly to bury Josy's German uniform and the rest of his army equipment well out of harm's way in the garden that night.

At eight o'clock the neighbors turned up as usual to listen to the BBC. In the meantime the miller's wife brought Josy some food and asked him not to walk around at night as the floors were old and squeaked when walked on. Emil woke up for a moment, blinked sleepily at Josy and then turned over and went back to sleep.

Josy wasn't really ready for sleep. There was too much on his mind. He sat on the twin bed he was to share with Tin and thought about his situation. He was happy to be in a safe haven and to have got away from the Germans, but he had no idea what the future held for him. The boy in the next bed worried him too. Would he, Josy wondered, give him away one day?

He became even more apprehensive as he looked around. There was no way of escape. What if the Germans came? How would he get away? He couldn't put the mill at risk. He knew that farmers from all around came with their horse-drawn wagons to have their grain milled, not only for their own families but also for undercover delivery all over the country.

Earlier, he'd been told, a boy from the south of the country had been hidden at the mill but had cracked under the strain and left. He also knew the miller supplied the flour for bread for the Luxembourg boys of conscription age hidden from the Germans in the forest of "Hondsbësch" (the dogs' forest) in Differdange. He could endanger the entire network. A shudder ran down his back.

Around midnight, after the guests had left, the miller locked all the doors and brought Josy down into the living-room, where they discussed their future plan of action. The miller reassured Josy that Emil was going to be the least of their problems. From the age of nine he knew what was happening in his country as his father had explained everything to him and he could be completely relied upon to keep his mouth shut. In fact, in the years that followed, he was to prove to be the best watchdog of the mill.

To provide Josy with somewhere to hide in case the Germans paid them an unexpected visit, the miller decided to install a second hiding-place over the cow stable in the hay loft. He wasted no time and started work right away, with the help of Tin, and by morning they had built a bunker of hay in the middle of the loft. Josy wasted no time either. As soon as the bunker was ready, he immediately started training, learning to get through the little hole in the ceiling as quickly as possible and take refuge in the haystack, where he could remain quietly in the dark.

The only remaining problem was the gable wall between Josy's room and his new hiding-place. If the Germans came suddenly, he would still be trapped. The only way out then would be the pistol he always carried round with him. The mill-pond would take care of the rest. An awful prospect, but war is a messy business and the brave people at the mill were prepared to face the consequences of what they were doing.

A couple of days later the German police called at Josy's parents' house in Oberanven. Both father and mother put on a show of being shocked and distraught when they were told that their son had not arrived at the base at Regensburg. They showed the policemen a card Josy had written personally. It read 'Greetings from Frankfurt' and carried the postmark of 16 February.

As Frankfurt was being very heavily bombed at the time, the Germans immediately concluded that their son must have been killed in an air raid on the city and said what they thought. Josy's parents looked deeply shocked and acted as though they were terribly upset. It was a clever ruse, as the card had been posted by Tin, who had gone to Germany to visit Luxembourgers deported to Germany. But it completely fooled the Germans. For them the Josy Puetz affair was closed.

In the meantime Josy was getting used to living in his new hiding place. It wasn't easy to remain all day long in a single room, but when he thought of the alternative, the living hell of the Russian front, he knew where he was better off.

To pass the time he read books and checked the accounts of the mill as well as peeling the potatoes and cleaning the vegetables for the miller's wife. He also rolled about 40 cigarettes a day for the miller, whose ready stocks of flour for bartering purposes ensured that, unlike many of his compatriots, he never went short of tobacco.

Towards the evening, when the pace of life slackened off a little, Josy would play games with Emil, but of course they had to make sure they didn't make any noise. Later on at night, when no deliveries were made to the mill and everybody in the village was safely tucked up in bed, Josy would take a walk outside, keeping well behind the mill, to get some fresh country air and much-needed exercise.

The days and weeks passed slowly by, but still there was no telling when the war would end. He spent most the days lying on his bed and gazing at the ceiling or counting the flowers on the wallpaper. He just had to be patient and stop himself from becoming depressed.

But his boredom was somewhat rudely shattered by two incidents that could have ended in disaster. Once when a cow had calved and he had been asked to help, he rushed into the kitchen to get a bowl of warm water only to find himself, hands and arms covered in blood, face to face with the postman. It is difficult to say who received the greater shock. Fortunately the postman, Mr. May of Roodt, kept his head, placed the newspaper on the table and walked out without saying a word.

The other time Josy was on the toilet when the German water control officials called, but he stayed where he was as quiet as a mouse. Again good fortune was on his side. The Germans didn't notice a thing.

The only local inhabitant who actually knew what was going on was the priest, Father Wiltzius, who had come to the mill to hear Josy's Easter confession. But he could be absolutely trusted and, in any case, there was no danger of a priest betraying the confidentiality of the confession.

Shortly afterwards, however, on a peaceful Sunday morning, they all came perilously close to disaster. Suddenly, without warning, the Gestapo appeared at the mill. No one had the slightest inkling of an idea they were coming. They had picked up Emil's father, Tin, who was on his usual Sunday morning walk near the mill. They suspected him of trading arms and took him with them to the mill, where they thought he might have hidden them.

The miller's wife was busy cooking and Josy was shaving at the kitchen sink beside the window when Emil, who had spotted the Gestapo escorting his father to the mill, rushed in to warn of the approaching danger.

In a flash Josy had disappeared from the kitchen through the roof cellar into the stable and his haystack hiding-place. Emil ran into the living-room and set the radio to the Berlin frequency while the miller's wife remained at the stove frying her rabbit. Molli the dog rushed to the door barking at the two Germans. Tin came in with them and had to take them up to Emil's room. He feared the worst. To his immense relief, he found it empty. Thank God!

Tin stood in front of the nightstand while one agent pulled the beds apart and the other searched the closet. While they were busy looking elsewhere, Tin was able to ease open the drawer and slip his revolver into his pocket. He breathed a sigh of relief. Now at least one piece of incriminating evidence had been eliminated.

Drawing: Filipe Da Costa

The Gestapo agents then turned to the very nightstand from which Tin had just removed his revolver. They rifled through the dresser, searched the miller's bedroom and then went down to the living room and the kitchen. Then they left for the mill. . . .

First they checked the chicken coop, setting all the silly birds squawking and flapping around, then the stable and finally, and almost catastrophically, climbed up to the hayloft itself. But they just searched through the hay they were standing on and found nothing suspect. After another hour they finally left, to everyone's tremendous relief.

When the miller came home from Sunday service a little later, he immediately realized something out of the ordinary had happened. In front of his wife's statues of saints, candles had been lit, while Josy, who had by then emerged from his place of refuge, was as white as a sheet. As for Emil, the hero of the hour, he was as proud as a young cockerel – and with good reason for he had saved them all.

When the miller heard what a close call they had all had, he shuddered. His wife served the soup, but no one had any appetite. They were still recovering from the miracle of their escape. They were certain that someone somewhere had prayed for them or, as we say in Luxembourg, 'a good nun had prayed for them.'

15 THE LAND OF RABBITS

IN THE SPRING OF 1991 I saw a little girl buying some hay for her rabbit in a local pet shop. Nothing unusual about that and I would have passed on by had I not noticed the exorbitant price on the transparent plastic bag that served as the packaging. My mind went back to our rabbits, my brother's and mine, when we were children during the war. It made me realize how times had changed. For all of us – people and rabbits.

My interest aroused, I soon started talking to the girl. She was only too happy to tell me all about her beloved rabbit, a thoroughbred silver-gray with white paws, called Fritz. Only the best, she beamed, was good enough for him. Well, we loved our rabbits too, but things were a little tougher for them.

In those harsh times they were fed whatever was available, but thrived on it all the same. Oddly enough, the Germans seemed to have overlooked rabbits. They were not included in the wartime animal count and their meat was not rationed.

Naturally almost every family raised rabbits during the war, and you could find them in barns, stables, shacks and even in town, where people kept them on balconies, and they appeared without fail as the principal dish on the Sunday menu of most households in the country. You could almost say that the Luxembourg wartime economy was based on rabbits.

One day we received a lovely brown-and-white spotted one as a gift from a neighboring family. At once my father set about building a wooden pen with doors made from left over wire netting. He placed it under the chicken coop and next to the pigsty.

To our delight our rabbit very soon surprised us with a litter of furry little newcomers, which crawled out of their nest after about a week and gathered round their mother to feed from her. When we went to touch them, the mother would jump towards us with an angry squealing sound and if we kept on she'd scratch and bite us. But the sweet little things soon got used to us and soon started scrambling across whenever we gave them a bowl of bread soaked in milk.

For us children there was nothing more important than the rabbits. We would spend hours with them. And whenever a rabbit somewhere had young ones we knew right away where it was and rushed there to look at them.

Competition among neighboring children was naturally fierce. We all thought that our own rabbits were the prettiest. One child would be bragging about her silver grays, another of his beautiful wild-looking browns and one boy even had a white one with red eyes. Our friend Pir was proud of his jet-black one and Jull of his strutting great male. I still remember clever Max, who would stand on his hind legs every time we whistled.

Under the prevailing Nazi laws, some of the names we gave the rabbits were clearly seditious, such as Ribbentrop, which we called the rabbit at the mill after the Nazi ambassador, and Kratzenberg, Luxembourg's notorious Gauleiter's right-hand man, whose name we bestowed on a poor unfortunate rabbit whose yellowish coat reminded us of the hated yellow Nazi uniforms worn by Luxembourg traitors, the 'Gielemaenecher.' We even named two rabbits after two German clowns and jokers, Tinnes and Scheel, who were famous in Cologne for the new jokes they were always coming up with.

We kept these names to ourselves, of course, or we'd have been in serious trouble with the Nazis.

Our young rabbits grew fast. After a couple of weeks there was no more room in our single pen, and our father built a few more. They were placed at the back of the house next to the cellar. Now they needed loads of food, and this is where we children had to show how much we cared for our rabbits – by working hard for them.

In spring we went into the fields and picked sappy dandelions and in summer we went into the meadows to fill our baskets with fresh and juicy grass and young clover, all mixed with cabbage leaves and carrots from the garden. In winter they lived on beet and oats. In the evening we covered them with hay and in the morning gave them dried bread or potato peelings mixed with oats. We just loved watching them munching away and looking up at us with their beady little black eyes.

Drawing: Marie-Josée Moreira

Since we fed our rabbits well, they quickly grew big and fat. That's when they were slaughtered. It always upset us when father took one out, held it up by the hind legs and hit it behind the head. We even had tears in our eyes as we watched its fur being pulled off.

The dead rabbit still had to hang for two days in the cellar and then it was chopped up into separate portions and roasted on Sundays. Mother varied the diet, cooking either with white sauce or with brown, sometimes fried, sometimes pickled or grilled. Nevertheless, as can be imagined, by the end of the war most people were fed up to the back teeth with eating rabbit.

During that time, however, rabbits didn't serve only as food. They were a much sought-after article of trade or barter. With the 'currency' of rabbits you could 'buy' many other things you needed. This is how my parents got my brother kitted out for his first communion, and the city hat-maker too got a rabbit in exchange for my mother's lovely new felt hat decorated with a bird of paradise on top.

Not much, however, could be made of rabbit fur. Some was treated and used in the lining of coats or cut to fit shoes to keep the feet warm, but fur coats and jackets made of rabbit skin were not yet in fashion at that time.

From time to time an old beggar woman from the 'Kalebierg,' a slum quarter of the town of Grevenmacher, came to the village to collect the skins that had been stuffed with hay after the slaughtering. I still remember her strangely melodious cry of 'Furs, furs!' ringing through the streets and I shall never forget her awful skinny dogs.

Not only did I feel sorry for her but also for those poor dogs, with their tongues hanging out as they pulled her cart up the hill. More than once I was told off at home because I had run after the team and helped her push the cart up the hill all the way to the last house in the village.

Rabbits may have been a lot of fun for us children, but we had to take care to look after them properly to make sure we kept them safe from disease or the ever-present danger, especially with rabbits, of inbreeding. Which reminds me of one occasion when my brother and I didn't know anything about that.

Mother had gone to Luxembourg City, so we decided to clean out the rabbit pens. Because the weather was nice we let some of the rabbits run loose on the hill behind the house. Then we sat watching them frolicking happily away in the fresh grass. We were really enjoying it all.

Suddenly Baach Jang, a railway-man who was on duty at the nearby railway level crossing, waved frantically at us, pointing at the male out of the pen. Whatever did he want, we wondered. We couldn't see anything wrong. So we just carried on having a good time – and, unfortunately for us, so did the rabbits.

We put them back in the pens before mother got back from town. When she learned what we had done, she told us off, but we didn't understand what we had done wrong. A couple of weeks later we did.

Two of the rabbits pulled out their wool and made a nest in the far corner of their pen. When the litter was born, mother called a neighbor to help. He arrived with a sack and we had to stay inside. When we fed the rabbits in the evening, we noticed that Nuckes and Schnuckes didn't want to come out to eat. Their little ones had disappeared. In our innocence we were the unwitting occasion of their grief. They were sad for quite some time. So were we.

16 WHEN CHICKENS RULED THE ROOST

CHICKENS RANKED WITH RABBITS as a key source of food during the war years. Any Luxembourger with more than half a dozen of his own had to notify the animal count office. It wasn't just the chickens that were so precious to the Germans but also the eggs they produced, and those eggs had to be delivered each week to a central location for transportation to towns in Luxembourg and Germany, the greater proportion of course going to Germany.

The Germans were not too precise in their count of chickens and eggs, simply estimating the average number of eggs each chicken was expected to lay and insisting that that amount had to be delivered. No one in Luxembourg tried to get round this law. It simply wasn't worth being caught for something so trivial, because the consequences would have been out of all proportion to the offence.

The half a dozen chickens we officially kept at home didn't need to be declared. Our problem was to find enough corn and grain to feed them, as well as the other half dozen we raised ourselves and kept very quiet about. Father solved the problem by working part time for the local farmers on his days off, harvesting their wheat and doing other odd jobs for them. That way we were able to feed our chickens and keep plenty of eggs for ourselves too. And every once in a while, a nice fat chicken would land happily in the pot.

As a result chickens and eggs were as precious as gold in Luxembourg during the war years. Town people would willingly trek many miles over country roads for any chance of getting them. Faced with such unremitting demand, we had to provide a continual supply of new young chickens and roosters in order to keep some of the produce for ourselves.

It was not as easy then to raise chicks as it is today. As soon as a chicken sat on an egg, we started to busy ourselves. We first gathered a few eggs for mother to check in the light of a candle to see whether they were fertile and when we found one we made a nest from a box. Now came the hard part, making the chicken sit on the egg, which was after all our idea, not the chicken's. If she wouldn't cooperate, we simply stuck a potato basket upside-down over the nest and left her to get on with it. As there was nothing else to do but sit on the egg, that's what the chicken would normally do. Except, oddly enough, on nights when the moon was full. Then she would lose all her motherly instincts and trample all over the eggs and crush them.

But most of the time the chicken would behave and sit patiently on her eggs. For our part, to ensure she didn't go hungry, we would place water and grain next to the box. It would take our hen three weeks to hatch her eggs. During that time only mother would be allowed to go up into the attic to make sure that everything was all right.

We knew when it was time for the eggs to hatch because the chicken would start to get restless, cackling and scratching, while pecking a hole in one of the eggs. Then a pathetic little squeak would be heard as a tiny chick began to struggle its way into the world out of its eggshell. Then came a second, then a third, and the exodus was under way.

As soon as mother heard the cackling and the squeaking, she would rush to get a basket, line it with linen, go up into the attic and take the wet little chicks and place them in the basket. This procedure would always upset the hen, who would cackle furiously away, until mother calmed her down by leaving one or two chicks with her while she was still sitting on the rest of the un-hatched eggs.

Mother would then carry the basket with the chicks downstairs and place it on the oven of the wood-burning stove, leaving the door open. The warmth was just what they needed. Their wet down, soon dried out and fluffed up, making them look like soft little yellow balls. As for us children, we couldn't see enough of the chicks and sometimes I would be allowed to pick one up. Then I loved nothing better than cuddling it close to my cheek. Once I put one on the floor, not realizing that its legs at that stage were too weak to walk. It started squeaking away and I hastily put it back in the basket.

During the days that followed, more chicks came down and went into the basket. The dry chicks were then transferred to a cardboard box and little by little more and more of them were able to stand on their own two feet.

One afternoon we went to see a hen in the attic. All the chicks were then out of the shell, though one still had a piece of shell stuck on its back. Before we put the remaining chicks in the basket to take downstairs, mother had to place the potato basket over the hen and secure it with a heavy pot to stop her from kicking up a fuss. As soon as we got the chicks downstairs, we put all the wet newly born into the warming basket on the oven and those that could run into a pen in the chicken coop.

Then mother went up and got the hen, which was by this time in a state of great agitation, her feathers fluffing up all over in her distress. But she soon calmed down when she saw her little babies in the pen. We gave her some milk and a scattering of breadcrumbs and then left them alone.

At around three in the afternoon we went to see them again. The chicks were happily milling round the hen, and mother somehow managed to make a head count of the constantly moving flock. There were 14. All of them had hatched and all looked healthy.

The hen took some breadcrumbs in her beak and deposited them in the open beaks of the chicks that hadn't yet helped themselves. It was fascinating to watch. As small as they were, they were already scrapping over a bite. Then all of a sudden the hen cackled and lifted her wings and the chicks all ran under to hide, but not for long. Some of them soon plucked up their courage and poked out their little heads to a chorus of pathetic little squeaks. It was a joy to hear.

For two days the hen and her brood had to stay in the pen. Then mother began to let them out on warm afternoons, when the hen would take them for a walk round the house. We had to be careful they didn't wander out into the road. Next we started feeding them on rice, which they gobbled up gratefully, with the hen watching over them like a sentry. She was the perfect mother. She didn't take her eye off them for one moment and would let no one approach them.

A week later they had outgrown the pen and were moved to a shack. With the door open and some fresh straw for them to dig and scratch into, they were in paradise and, my goodness, how quickly they grew! You could almost see them getting bigger. Before long we could make out the little roosters, with their proud combs and long hind feathers. Mother counted six of them and she was more than happy with that. Six roosters were more than enough to keep the hens happy and ensure there would be plenty more chicks on the way.

Then it was decided that the chicks were to be fed twice a day. Two days later something went horribly wrong. I don't remember exactly what happened, but while I was feeding them the board that held the door open fell down and landed right on the chicks. The hen squawked and flew into the corner of the room, while three or four of the chicks ran around in a panic, squeaking loudly. All the others had disappeared. I was rooted to the spot, paralysed with fear. Finally I plucked up my courage and lifted up the board and there lay my lovely little chicks – all dead.

I turned and ran down by the rail tracks, down by the hill, and hid in the lowest part of our garden. I threw myself to the ground and sobbed my heart out. As I lay there a train raced by. On the other side of the Syr, the village lay peacefully. The water flowed quietly by and Knuppen's geese were chattering happily away down below.

But that all passed me by. Tears were streaming down my face and my nose was running. I couldn't go home like this. What was I to do? I remained sitting there, probably an hour or two - it seemed like forever. All of a sudden the five-thirty train roared by. Now I knew what I had to do. I had to go home and tell my mother everything.

But when I got there it was too late. Mother had already discovered what had happened and was in tears. She took me to the shack and showed me the dead chicks. On top of everything else it was all too much for me. I burst into tears again, ran into the house and up the stairs to hide away on my bed.

Mother simply thought I felt sorry for the chicks and had no idea that I had caused the accident in the first place. All sorts of possible causes were endlessly discussed and everyone who came to the house was told about it. I felt awful. Like a murderer.

As the evening bells began to toll in the church, my brother Marcel came in from the village. That set my mother off crying again. Naturally he wanted to see the dead chicks, but it was too late – they had already been buried. He then came up to my room to see how I was getting on. Mother followed close behind and insisted that I went down and ate some supper.

At the table mother's tears began to flow again. She went on about how hard she had worked to raise such lovely little chicks, how we would no longer have any young chickens next year to lay more eggs than the old ones, no little roosters, no chickens to eat, and that it was too late now for any of our chickens to raise another litter this year. My sandwich got stuck in my throat. I felt so bad. I had intended to tell the truth before I went to bed, but now I was too scared.

I slept badly all that night and next morning at school the problem was still tormenting me. In the afternoon I was hardly able to concentrate on my private French lessons at the house of my teacher, Mr. Jakoby, and made a lot of mistakes. He wondered what was wrong with me, and I found myself on the verge of telling him.

When I got home, mother looked at me strangely. My heart felt as though it was about to burst out of my chest and I must have gone white in the face. She must have suspected something. 'When did you last see the chicks?' she asked.

That was the last straw. I broke down sobbing and went down on my knees in front of her and told her it was all my fault. She looked puzzled and simply said: 'Why didn't you tell me this right away?'

I couldn't stop crying and didn't reply, but mother didn't do anything, except to say she was surprised I had done this. To my enormous relief I wasn't punished or even told off. All she said was that I was lucky my father hadn't been at home and that when he did return next Saturday she was not going to say a word about what had really happened.

The next day she called on the 'godmother,' the miller's wife, and when I got home from school our hen was proudly strutting around with a dozen chicks again. They were from the same family as our unfortunate little ones, cousins in fact. She had contentedly tucked them all under her own wings as though they were her own.

What had happened? Need I say? The dear 'godmother' had saved the day as she had so many times in the past already. She had taken eight chicks away from her own two hens and given them to my mother to take home. The wound had been healed.

But I didn't get away with it altogether. After our midday meal next day my mother and I had a long chat – and my mother did all the talking.

17 AN ACT OF DEFIANCE

1943 ... 1944 ... IT SEEMED TO GO ON and on . . . how much longer, we prayed, were we to endure occupation by the Nazi forces of Adolf Hitler. Many of our people languished in German prisons while others were being tortured and killed in German concentration camps.

The hated political leader or 'Gauleiter' of our country, the Nazi boss and traitor Gustav Simon, ruled with a rod of iron and conscripted our young men into service in the German army, where many of them were to lose their lives fighting against their will on the side of their country's enemy in Russia or some other theatre of war where the Germans were now falling back in headlong retreat and disarray.

Everywhere the story was the same. Some of our young men resisted the German forced conscription and joined the underground resistance, the "Maquis," while yet others hid in forests and secret places prepared by their families and friends, thereby endangering their own lives and those of the people who protected them.

The Germans had no pity for those they caught. People were being deported to Germany in large numbers and nobody involved in anti-Nazi activities knew when they were going to hear that dreaded knocking at the door. So many people lived in constant fear. It was a time of anguish and depression for Luxembourg.

In the meantime ministers sent messages of hope and encouragement via the BBC from their safe haven in London. But it was easy for them to talk. They were well out of the danger zone. In any case most of us, face to face with the reality of Germany occupation, were sick to death of our politicians' empty talk by then and were not impressed. They just made us mad.

It was different, however, when the voice of Her Royal Highness the Grand Duchess Charlotte came across the airwaves, strong and ringing with sincerity. She really was able to convince us that one day we would all be free again. In our heart of hearts we believed every word she said, but in the meantime we could hardly wait to be rid of the Germans, whose occupation of our country bore down more heavily on us day by day.

In those hard cruel times it was above all our Catholic Faith that kept our hopes alive. We would certainly have lost heart had it not been for our strong and firm belief and closeness in prayer to the patron saint of our country, the Blessed Virgin Mary, our 'Consolatrix Afflictorum' (Consoler of the Afflicted). We passed all our distress and worries on to her and thereby eased the burden we had to bear.

Each day many Luxembourgers walked to the cathedral and knelt before the statue of our Lady of Luxembourg. Her picture had the place of honour in our homes, in the bunkers on the front lines, in prisons and concentration camps and was taken into deportation.

And she didn't fail us. Through our prayers and faith she gave us the strength and courage we needed to endure the suffering the Prussians inflicted on us. Thus we struggled on through those dark and difficult times. Somehow we found an identity, a unity and a common cause we did not realize we had. That, we believed, and still do, was God's answer, through His Holy Mother, to our prayers.

But it was during Luxembourg's traditional two-week pilgrimage known as the Octave that our newfound resistance to the invader was really put to the test.

The Nazis swarmed all round us then doing all they could to block and hinder the traditional processions of pilgrims walking from villages all over the country to the Cathedral of Our Lady in the city of Luxembourg. They made the observance of the Octave almost impossible. Pilgrim trains were cancelled and official processions were forbidden by the Nazi-law. No more than about 12 people were allowed to march in procession at any one time and it was declared illegal to pray aloud in public in either the villages or the city.

When the air raid sirens sounded the doors of the cathedral were locked and worshippers herded off like cattle to the underground caves known as the casemates until the air raid was over. If the raids took place at night – which usually happened – the doors of the cathedral remained locked until 10 o'clock the following morning.

But the religious community fought back, despite the fearful prohibitions imposed by the Nazis, and somehow enough worshippers always found a way to get into the cathedral and celebrate the Octave Mass.

Luxembourgers thereby succeeded in upholding the sacred tradition of honoring the promise made by their ancestors to Our Lady of Luxembourg. And not only in Luxembourg City. At the same time, as if by some mystical or synchronistic collective command, the Octave was similarly celebrated in every village church throughout the land, including our own little village of Olingen.

I well remember how excited our new priest, Father Wiltzius, was about celebrating the Octave in his first parish. Somehow, equipped with nothing more than a harmonium and his own contagious enthusiasm, he managed to organize us village children into a children's choir, which, in view of the local talent available, must have itself been something of a miracle. Fired by his fervor and boosted by his belief in us, we were only too pleased to practice Luxembourg hymns in his house a couple of times a week.

The week before the Octave Sunday the church was a hive of activity, with a host of willing workers polishing the bells, the incense vessel and the candelabra. The choirboys erected a special altar, which the priest's housekeeper decorated with blue silk and carpets, while we girls of the village busied ourselves preparing the crown, the sceptre and the key for the statue of Our Lady of Luxembourg, which had been clothed in a beautiful shimmering dress.

Drawing: Paula Antunes

When it was all finished we gazed with awe and wonder at the result of our labors. The church had been transformed. We then ran through the village and gathered as many flowers as we could to adorn the church with what really amounted to a defiant display of the national colors of Luxembourg - a gorgeous array of blue and white forget-me-nots and red tulips. Our statement of resistance had been made. Now the Octave could begin.

Despite the Nazi disapproval of our Octave celebrations and the threat it implied, the church was full. For two weeks the Octave was celebrated each day in that church. Everybody in the village who could go was there. Traditional Octave songs had been forbidden by the Nazi-authorities, but we fooled them by singing other popular hymns.

My children's choir sang each morning without fail at the 'Ave spes nostra' Mass and the church was packed to the rafters for every evening service that week. Many of the hymns were deeply nostalgic, particularly the Laurentic Litanies, where, under the baton of our gifted conductor, Ziirden Albert, the choir sang 'Consolatrix Afflictorum, ora pro nobis' with great feeling. These hymns struck a chord in the hearts of more than a few of the older people, who could be seen wiping a tear or two from their eyes.

The secret excitement of defying all the efforts of our Nazi rulers to suppress our acts of worship and the sheer joy of the occasion lifted the brutal fact of Nazi occupation from our minds.

At last the day dawned when everyone was expected to go on the annual pilgrimage to the city to attend the Octave Mass in the cathedral and most of us did, even though, lots of obstacles had been put in our way by the occupiers.

My mother took me too, and we left very early at 5.30 in the morning. On our way we prayed loudly for our former priest, who was in the notorious Dachau concentration camp, and my friend Alice walked and prayed for her brother, who had been conscripted into the German army and was fighting for his life somewhere in Russia. We walked quietly through the villages, praying silently by ourselves for our loved ones and our country. We all knew why we were going.

It was early morning by the time we arrived at Findel, on the outskirts of the city. The Germans military seemed to be everywhere. Several passed us on motorbikes with sidecars and looked at us angrily. They well knew our religious procession was more than it seemed, a form of silent insubordination, an act of defiance. So to keep out of trouble, we walked in Indian file along the side of the road. We had to stop praying aloud when we reached the suburb of Neudorf, on the city's very edge, and soon, to our relief and joy, the towers of the cathedral came into view.

As we crossed the castle bridge of the 'Bock' (the birthplace or cradle of both the city and the country, the very site where Luxembourg first began to take form in the 10th century) we looked down into the valley and saw the prison, with the Luxembourgish political prisoners, most of them underground resistance members taking their daily walk in the courtyard. We could almost feel their desperation. The priest's housekeeper started to cry and many of us had lumps in our throats.

The city felt empty. Spiritually empty. The Octave feeling was no longer there. In front of the grand-ducal palace had been desecrated by ugly swastika flags and every corner had its small contingents of German troops, watching everything and everybody. The people were massing outside the cathedral, waiting to go in, but German troops stood guard on all the doors. No one said a word. We just waited.

Then at last at 10 o'clock our patience was rewarded, the huge gates swung open and we all poured in, expecting to be packed together like cattle in a truck. But inside there appeared to be plenty of room, and everyone in the vast crowd, almost miraculously, found a place.

'Our Lady of Luxembourg,' cascaded with flowers, stood on the votive altar, and everyone seemed to be gazing silently at her. But the lighting was poor and the mood was somber. The organ, however, played beautifully and the people knelt in front of the altar and poured out their hearts in prayer.

All of a sudden, even as a child, I realized what a terrible burden the people had been carrying and, more importantly, what it actually meant to carry a cross.

I realized too how lucky we were in our small village church in Olingen to be able to fully and joyfully celebrate the Octave there. Every morning for two weeks we assisted at a special 'Ave spes nostra' Mass, where we were joined in prayer and worship by every villager able to be there.

The memories of those two happy weeks, singing our little hearts out in the church choir, remain with me till this very day.

18 'GOOD LITTLE ANGEL'

EVERY DARK CLOUD HAS A SILVER LINING and many good things happen in hard times. Luxembourgers are normally reserved people and like to keep to themselves. Like the suspicious peasants they once were, invaded and occupied by foreign powers throughout almost their entire history, they protect their privacy like a dog guarding a bone, but during the war years that all changed.

Then they came together in a way they hadn't done in living memory, sticking together like glue, everyone only too anxious to help out whenever anyone else was in need. Which is how I came to get my wartime job.

At home in Olingen we never forgot our friends living in the city and, as a young girl, I played a part in maintaining those links. For two years I traveled regularly to town, carrying supplies of food for two families who were friends of ours, the Jacquemarts and the Arnoldys.

On the afternoons when there was no school I walked from Olingen to Roodt, where I caught the train to the Luxembourg City. Most of the time I was carrying a dozen or so eggs, a pound each of butter and flour and some vegetables from the garden. We used to get the eggs, butter and flour from neighboring farmers, who gave them to us in exchange for the work we did on their farms.

For my poor mother it wasn't just the hard work that got her down. It was also the precious time she had to waste in the company of nosey old farmers' wives who wanted to know all our business before they would let her have the food she needed to help feed our city friends.

It didn't take long to find my way around the city. First I had to walk from the station along the Old Avenue or 'Bahnhofsstrasse' (railway station road) as the Germans renamed it. I then took the road leading to the city milk-processing plant (years later converted into the administrative headquarter of the 'Farmers' Centrale') to finally arrive at the Jacquemart residence.

Mrs. Jacquemart was always happy to see me with my bag full of food and called me their 'good little angel.' But even at that tender age I realized it wasn't just my smiling face that inspired them to award me my angelic status!

As soon as I arrived Mrs. Jacquemart rewarded me with a glass of home-made raspberry juice or some such similar treat. I am sure she would have done that anyway, not just for the provisions we were able to give her, for she never failed to make a fuss of her housemaid, Kathy, whenever she brought food back from the weekends she spent with her family at her home farming village. Mrs. Jacquemart was just simply a lovely generous lady.

But what fascinated me most were the interesting stories she used to tell me about times past in Luxembourg, when, for example, my grandfather used to come from the Moselle village of Greiveldingen by horse and wagon to deliver wine to their hotel.

Then she told me about her son, Josy, whom the Germans had thrown into prison for his underground resistance activities, and about Theo, her son's best friend, who had moved in with her so she wouldn't have to have a German officer billeted on her.

It was quite bad enough, she told me, having to put up with German police living next door in the Sacred Heart Monastery, which had formerly been run by Luxembourg monks who had fled to southern France. She looked upon these 'neighbors' as little more than spies.

I knew that Mrs. Jacquemart was a sophisticated city lady and that my simple country bumpkin ways often used to amuse her. But as she was such a nice person I didn't mind her laughing at me now and then. In any case what I really used to enjoy was going to town afterwards and window-shopping along the main city streets. For a child who lived in a village that was a real treat.

During the holidays I went in the mornings, when I was able to take more food provisions as the police weren't around to check up on what people were carrying. Afterwards I would stay for lunch with the Jacquemarts.

I just loved being there in that big city house, because everything was handled differently, nicer somehow, than in our pokey little village home. It was the class and style, of course, but I really had no idea at the time. I only knew that I liked it and felt as though I was on holiday. Naturally I was always on my best behavior and learned a lot more about good manners and gracious living while I was there.

The major worry in Mrs. Jacquemart's life was the imprisonment of her son, Josy. She just lived for the visiting days, when she took eggs, butter, sausage sandwiches and whatever she could get for Josy and his fellow prisoners.

She got away with getting those extra rations to her son because she had managed to bribe one of the guards, who consequently ended up with a fair amount of our food in his belly, but she didn't care about that as long as Josy got a bit more than the meager prison ration. Which was why she was so anxious to receive the extra food I brought her each week.

One morning Mrs. Jacquemart took me for a walk along Luxembourg's scenic path, a sort of cliff-top route known as the "Corniche" that runs round one side of the beautiful scenic valley that divides the original historical city of Luxembourg from the main railway station area.

It was the first time I had been in that part of the city. The view is magnificent, spanned by the great bridges that join the old city to the new with lovely green parks and the picturesque area known as the Grund stretching out down below.

But all Mrs. Jacquemart had eyes for that morning was the prison, which was the real reason for her little excursion. She simply wanted to see her son for the all-too-brief period prisoners were let out into the yard for their daily exercise.

We took up our position at the high point near the Bock (the rock on which the Count Siegfried built his castle in AD 963, the foundation of the city of Luxembourg), gazing down into the prison yard and waiting alongside a dozen or so other Luxembourgers there for the same purpose.

Eventually, about 10 o'clock, the prisoners appeared, dressed in their prison uniforms and closely guarded, and started circling round the yard for the next quarter-of-an-hour. All of us on the Corniche began waving handkerchiefs, gesturing and making all sorts of signs.

Mrs. Jacquemart recognized her son right away because he blew his nose and rubbed his hand over his head. It was their personal signal. I guess almost all the prisoners and their families had similar codes.

Everyone stayed there, never taking their eyes off their loved ones down below, until at length the prisoners were herded back inside. Then many of them, including Mrs. Jacquemart, started weeping quietly while others sadly looked on.

Drawing: João Gomes

It was an experience I have never been able to forget. As the prison gates closed again those people who had come along went home with at least one important consolation – they knew their loved ones hadn't yet been cast into the hell of a Nazi concentration camp.

The other family I kept supplied with food lived in the 'Rosegarden' in Hollerich, in the newer part of the city. My mother went with me on my first two trips, as it was more difficult to find their house. To get there I had to go up the New Avenue past a magnificent building covered in Nazi flags, which was and still is today the seat of the famous Luxembourg steel company, Arbed, nowadays Arcelor, but then was the headquarters of Luxembourg's Gauleiter, Hitler's representative in Luxembourg.

I carried on over the Adolphe or New Bridge until I reached a field hospital with Red Cross vehicles and German soldiers in the yard by the tall 'Convict' building. This diocesan property had been confiscated by the Nazis at the time, but before the war had been used as a boarding school for male students.

The last lap of my journey took me down the endless Esch road until I came to a butcher's shop on the corner of a small square where the Arnoldys lived.

There too I was always warmly welcomed as the bearer of good things, which Mrs. Arnoldy shared with relatives of hers who had been sentenced to deportation. She baked cakes from the produce I had brought her and sent them to the Nazi deportation camp at Leubus, Germany.

I got along well with her only daughter, Jacqueline, who was a year younger than I. During the holidays I once stayed with them for a couple of days. But everything at the Arnoldys, who lived in a second-floor apartment, was quite different from the style and splendor of the Jacquemarts. Nevertheless, I was impressed by the comfort they enjoyed, even though they had no garden or grass surroundings and their rabbits were confined to a pen on the balcony.

But Jacqueline had everything she could possibly need, including a playroom with several dolls, teddy bears, a 'doll's house' grocery store, a piano and a spinning top, which played music. But none of that held much interest for me. All I wanted to do was read her many books, which led her father to predict that I would grow up to be a teacher.

Not that I had much opportunity to read books at the Arnoldys. Jacqueline had other ideas. She was very sporting and was to become a physical education teacher when she herself grew up. She loved nothing better than to drag me off to the park to join her on the swings, which always made me feel dizzy and sick.

Her program also included swimming and roller-skating, neither of which I liked. At the swimming pool I spent most of the time watching her diving like a bird from the high board and swimming like a fish in the deep end. As for roller-skating, I could never master that, however hard I tried.

The only outdoor activity of hers I enjoyed was riding on our bicycles. We used to cycle all over the place and I really got to know the west part of the city that way, including the interesting rural area known as the 'Geesseknäppchen.'

Naturally my friends at school wanted to know what I was up to in the city every week, but I kept it all very much to myself. Some of them seemed to have guessed what was going on and tried to scare me with stories about spot police checks, but that didn't worry me. Nobody took much notice of innocent-looking little girls trotting through the streets. I would have made the perfect Mati Hari!

None the less on one occasion I was stopped, at Roodt railway station, but I must have led a charmed life in those days as luck was on my side. My bag contained nothing more than garden surplus, such as green beans, carrots, peas and salad, which my mother wanted to share with her friends in the city. Perfectly legitimate. So nothing was said.

But occasionally I did see people who were not so lucky and had their goods confiscated on the spot. For example, I shall never forget the poor woman who got into such a panic that she dropped all her eggs over a policeman's feet. I don't know whether she got arrested. I didn't stay to see.

Still, when you're a child you just don't realize the risks you are taking and I just carried blithely on, not even giving a second thought to what could have happened to me.

As time wore on I became a little careless and now and then wandered off my usual route in the city, curious to see as much as I could of our capital. Then one day, while I was walking along the main street known as the 'Groussgaass,' the air-raid sirens started to wail. Everyone started to panic. Almost at once the traffic ground to a halt. I just ran as fast as my little legs would carry me, hoping to reach the Jacquemarts' house before anything happened.

But it was too late. Just before I got there, German soldiers on the corner of the Old Avenue spotted me and herded me along with everyone else into the nearby air-raid shelters. There was nothing I could do. I was trapped.

Down I went into the dank dark caves dug into the rock on which the city was built and known as the 'casemates.' Lit by a single lamp, it was black and gloomy down there in what seemed to me like the bowels of the earth. I wasn't at all happy in the stale atmosphere, surrounded by people I didn't know.

The only thought that consoled me was that at least my mother wouldn't be worrying. The railway service would have phoned to tell her that the seven o'clock train had been held up by an air raid warning.

After a while I began to look around. Next to the exit from the caves stood a bank of sandbags, with shovels and picks propped up nearby against the cave walls beside barrels of fresh water. It looked as though preparations had been made for a long siege. Silly, I know, but my child's mind was prey to all sorts of fantasies and I began to wonder how long we were going to be kept in there.

Most of the people sat on wooden benches around the bunker with the soldiers next to them, but nobody said a word, perhaps in obedience to the notices on the walls or perhaps because they just didn't feel like it.

Then at last, just as the tension was becoming unbearable, the all-clear sirens burst into joyful song and we all streamed happily outside, with everyone chattering all at once. You could almost touch the sense of relief. I ran straight to the railway station, where my train stood waiting. It left some time later and I eventually arrived home to a warm and relieved welcome about half past eight.

My mother continued sending me to the Jacquemarts and Arnoldys with whatever food they could spare for some time after, but by May 1944, when wave after wave of allied bombers began to target the city with increasing frequency, my parents decided it was too dangerous for me to carry on.

Our city friends understood of course, but they had a hard time managing to get enough to eat, and even staying alive, in the fearful months that followed. But they made it, and they never forgot the help we gave them for as long as we could.

The following year, in April 1945, when I went to high school in the city, Mrs. Jacquemart insisted that I stay with her almost as a guest of honor in her lovely house as there was no room in the boarding school. Only the classrooms had been opened. The other part of the building was occupied by American soldiers for a further three months until October 1945.

I treasure the memory of those precious days. The friendships we forged in the crucible of Nazi occupation did not rust away. Ours lasted the lifetime of our parents — and we 'children' remain close to this very day.

19 A WORLD OF MAKE-BELIEVE

HARDLY A DAY PASSED during the occupation without the usual barrage of propaganda from the German radio and newspapers. Why they bothered I don't know, because no one believed a word of it. We all used to joke about those boastful broadcasts behind the Germans' backs, but walls have ears and sometimes word got round and someone had to pay a heavy price for our joking.

Their stupid propaganda was bad enough itself to put up with but far worse were the many ways we were forced into helping the German war effort. The hated 'Winterhilfswerk' (winter help action) immediately springs to mind. We had to take our turns going from house to house with a tin can on Sunday mornings to beg for money for German families in need because their fathers were fighting on the front line for Germany or their mothers away from home enthusiastically working for the Germans.

Humiliation was heaped on humiliation by the instruction to reward the sponsors by giving them pins supposedly to be worn as some sort of 'badge of honor' for the part they were playing in the German war effort. In fact they were seldom displayed by the sponsors, who knew only too well that most Luxembourgers looked upon the pins as 'badges of shame.' Only the children appreciated them, but children are children, wherever they are, and badges or decorations or any sort are always irresistible to them.

At first Luxembourgers flatly refused to take part in these collections for families sympathetic to the Nazi cause. But it wasn't as easy as that. The Nazis were notorious for their methods of 'persuading' people in their power to cooperate with them, however unwilling those people were.

They did so in this case by keeping lists of those of us who collected money for them, those who paid up and those who didn't, and those who point-blank refused to undergo the indignity of collecting money for an enemy that had invaded and occupied our country. The names of those unwilling to collect or contribute were added to a dreaded black list, which put them at serious risk of ending up in prison, being deported or sent to a concentration camp.

As a result we soon came to realize that resistance was futile and ended up paying reluctantly and going from door to door with heavy hearts whenever our turn came round. What else could we do? In those dreadful dark days of Nazi occupation, when the war seemed to be going their way and liberation was only a dream, all we wanted to do was to keep the Germans off our backs.

Nazi propaganda was of course slanted particularly to our children, whose school- books were crammed with words and pictures glorifying the Nazi ideology. They also organized events and demonstrations to ridicule the enemy, such as a display of pictures and posters held at the exhibition hall at Limpertsberg and entitled 'Soviet paradise,' which all the schools were obliged to visit.

I well remember how we traveled there on a cold day, by foot, train and tram, taking the whole day to do it. And all to see a crude mockery of Russia and the Russians, depicting them as savage and primitive people little changed since the time of Attila the Hun.

It was of course intended to instill a terrible fear of the Russians into our hearts – and it succeeded. We saw a couple of huts in an awful wilderness, with people and animals living under one roof. The place looked as filthy as a pigsty. Right next to it were drunks and robbers, who fought one another with swords and axes.

It all made a horrible impression on my young mind and for some time afterwards I firmly believed that the Russians, which the Germans always contemptuously referred to as Bolsheviks, were little better than wild animals.

In 1942, when Hitler's invading armies ground to a halt in the snows of Stalingrad, a collection of good warm clothing was organized in Luxembourg for the soldiers trapped there. The window of the Jacob shop at Roodt was filled with woolen clothing of almost every type, sweaters, scarves, shirts and socks, etc. In the middle sat a German soldier tailor's dummy dressed in warm white fatigues, with fur-lined boots, supposedly to represent a typical German soldier perfectly equipped for those awful Russian winter weather conditions and encourage us to keep them supplied with warm clothing.

The fur-lined boots particularly caught my attention. I wondered wryly how many soldiers in the German army, including our own young Luxembourg conscripts, were actually lucky enough to be as well protected by boots and clothing like that against the terrible Russian winter. I shuddered at the thought of the hell on earth those poor boys were going through.

But the Germans were not interested in the warm clothing on display in Jacob's other window, because they were only second-hand clothes. They only wanted the best. What was left over was fit only for Luxembourgers. They considered it beneath their dignity to wear the clothing we no longer wanted. They didn't realize their foolishness. Their poor soldiers on the Russian front would not have been so particular. They would have worn anything to keep warm in the cruel arctic conditions they were expected to fight and die in.

Although our own plight couldn't of course be compared with that of the soldiers facing the Red army at Stalingrad, we could certainly have done with some more warm clothing ourselves during that ice-age winter of 1942. Many houses were poorly heated as fuel was strictly rationed and we were allowed to collect only so much wood per household from the forest. We just had to make do with sticks, wherever we could find them. Coal was precious and had to be saved at all costs.

The Germans launched a fuel-saving campaign, sticking up posters everywhere of a cartoon figure they called the 'coal thief,' depicted as wagging his finger whenever we had left doors open or let the heat escape from open windows.

Another enemy of the German war effort was the 'potato beetle.' On certain days in the summer, to get rid of this beetle and save the potato crop, local villagers had to march in line across the potato fields and collect those ugly brown insects in tin cans. We children quite enjoyed it, especially when we got home and fed our unfortunate captives to the chickens. But after a while the chickens had had enough of the same dull old dish on the menu each day and wouldn't go near them. All we could do then was to throw the poor little creatures in the fire and watch them burn. All in the name of the German war effort. The Fuehrer would have been proud of us!

In the spring another of our chores was to collect 'tea' (i.e. herbs from the forests) for the soldiers on the front line and in the field hospitals. Again we had a lot of fun doing it, even though we didn't take it seriously.

Our teacher, Mr. Jakoby, wasn't quite so tolerant of what he called Prussian imbecilities. He knew we were falling behind in our schoolwork because of the time we had to waste on what amounted to little more than slave labor for the Germans. He also made no bones about how much he objected to the school garden we had to waste time working in to provide extra food for the Germans.

But Mr. Jakoby had an even stronger reason to hate the Germans. They had conscripted his only son into the German army and sent him to Russia. His thoughts, each day, were only for 'Roger,' who was more important to him than anything or anybody else. The Germans had abducted his only deeply loved son, who was also a brilliant scholar, and he certainly had no intention of helping them fight their war. Sadly he was never to see Roger again.

For us children the worst aspect of the Nazi propaganda was our enforced membership of the hated Hitler Youth ('Hitlerjugend'). Until 1942 we had largely managed to avoid it, but then the Germans ordered all workers and employees to enroll their children or face the consequences – and every Luxembourger knew what that meant. We then had to go once a week to the rallies at Roodt, where the local Hitler Youth meetings were held in the baker's house, which the Germans had confiscated after the Jewish baker had fled with his family

We children of Olingen were always being told off for being late, which we couldn't help as our new priest always gave catechism classes on the same afternoon. On top of that our priest didn't like us going to the Hitler Youth meetings, so we ended up in a classic catch-22 'heads we lose tails you win' situation, upsetting everyone, even the local farm boys, who accused us of collaboration!

That really made us angry and almost started gang warfare among the Olingen children. But the farm boys soon shut up when the deportations started and they quickly found themselves 'collaborating' with us on the road to Roodt every week.

All of us children from the villages of Roodt, Mensdorf and Olingen were taught German songs and shown films glorifying the Fuehrer and The Fatherland. The area leader kept a close eye on us and never stopped trying to brainwash us with promises of glories to come beyond our dreams in the paradise of a golden Nazi future.

In the summer of 1943 we had to start wearing a uniform, which for the girls among us consisted of a black skirt, a white blouse and a black scarf with a leather knot. Thus fully kitted out like little Nazis we had to endure the humiliation of marching through Roodt singing popular German songs like 'Westerwald' (Woods of the West) and 'Lueneburger Heide' (Heath-lands of Lueneburg'). Each time I saw someone I knew I felt myself going pink with embarrassment.

But slowly we started to learn a few tricks and find excuses not to go – a bad fall, a visit to the dentist, a stomach ache, a nose bleed, etc. You name them, we used them. We could keep that up for only so long of course and had to go along now and again.

On two occasions in the summer of 1944 the meetings were held in the castle at Betzdorf, where the Germans held a permanent camp called the 'Union of German girls.' A group of German girls led a good life there. Sometimes in summer they would organize a youth evening with attractive programs of entertaining games in the castle or outside in the park or forest, finishing off in the evening with a group sing-song round a campfire.

It wouldn't have been too bad really had it not been for the grim reality of Nazi propaganda behind all the fun we were having. In any case it was all a complete farce, for the Americans were getting closer every day and we could hardly wait for them to arrive.

When at last they did, the German girls disappeared overnight, fleeing in the direction of Germany, and we awoke to find ourselves rid of the entire repulsive charade of Nazi make-believe, lies and propaganda. What a relief! We were almost hysterical with joy. All we could do was fall on our knees and thank God.

20 TRAINED TO BE A GERMAN TEACHER

ON A HOT STEAMING DAY early in July 1944, I was preparing for an important journey. My two suitcases, one large and the other small, lay next to each other beside a schoolbag on the cart. My brother helped carrying the luggage from Olingen to Roodt and put it on the train. My father couldn't help us – he had been forced to work in Germany at the railway terminal of Ehrang. My mother went with me alone to Walferdange, just north of the city of Luxembourg.

I had finished my time at primary school and had decided I wanted to become a teacher, so I had to take an examination at the teachers' training school (known as the 'Lehrerinnen Bildungsanstalt' or LBA) at Walferdange. Why the luggage and all the fuss? Well, the examination was to last the whole week.

Along with us on the train was a group of young girls with their mothers or whoever was taking care of them. We all went in the same direction to the great park of the Château de Walferdange, where the Germans had established the school. As soon as we arrived, we were greeted by the excited chattering of a crowd of young girls. It was pandemonium.

But about 150 young girls, full-time students of the school in their uniforms of the Union of the Young German Girls, took care of us new arrivals and soon got everything under control. These girls, many of them German and most of them Nazis, were known as the Hitler girls. All instructions were given in the haughty superior German known as High German. Our first orders were to go to the office of the director to clear all the paperwork.

The time then came for us to be left on our own. My heart was heavy as my mother gave me her final words of advice and said her goodbyes. Away from home for the first time, I felt alone and lost among all those girls I didn't know. Many girls must have felt the same, but some of them talked big as though they already knew what the test was all about. I listened in wonderment, drinking in every word.

Our names were eventually called out and we were each given our place in the various bedrooms. My place was on the third floor, in the attic, in the middle building. It was a long room with about 30 beds in three long rows. The windows were so high that, even standing up, you couldn't see out of them. I still remember what a job it was to lug my cases up all those stairs.

I also remember how embarrassed I was when I opened them and discovered that they contained more food than clothes. My dear mother had packed a whole cake, several slices of ham, a glass of preserve, about a dozen hard-boiled eggs and many homemade biscuits.

When one of the Hitler girls spotted all that food, her eyes nearly popped out of her head and she immediately ordered me to remove all my 'rubbish food' from the room. A whole group of girls stood around gaping and grinning. I had tears in my eyes. I wished I was back home and couldn't keep from sobbing when I had to make my bed and put my clothes in the pokey little cupboard I shared with a couple of other girls.

Then another Hitler girl, Steffi, came along and took care of me and my food, which she allowed me to put in a locker next to the dining-room. I shall never forget Steffi. She was kind and sympathetic and made me feel much better. She also helped me later when I had some problems with the German drill.

The first major address took place before dinner in the evening after all the candidates had arrived and been placed. The school chief prefect or 'head leader,' as we called her, greeted us with 'Heil Hitler' and gave the Hitler salute, which we had to return.

She then gave a speech about the Fuehrer, Adolf Hitler. She had so many good things to say about this 'great friend' of German youth, which included, on the Fuehrer's orders, all young Luxembourgers. What's more, we would have to prove we were worthy of this friendship by true duty towards the Fuehrer, the people and the German Fatherland.

We had to applaud. We had no choice. But what really made me sick was the way some of the Luxembourg girls responded to the speech, cheering and clapping as though they had been listening to the Grand Duchess Charlotte herself.

Then we were told about the strict rules of the school and the tests. During supper I felt so sick about everything that I could hardly force the food down my throat. Afterwards we strolled through the beautiful park. I felt completely lost. In which direction, I wondered nostalgically, was my little village. I had to know. Already I felt terribly homesick.

Later in the dormitory we all felt a lot better and began to let our hair down. Then two of the Hitler girls who slept in the room with us came in and told us we had to wash from top to toe in the communal washroom – and, what's more, we had to do it in the nude.

Most of us timid younger ones were shocked by this order, but a few of the more fully developed girls were as bold as brass about it and seemed only too pleased to show off their bodies. Those of us who were shy were mocked as 'innocents of the country' ('country bumpkins' in English) and I was among them.

Once we were in bed the leaders checked to see whether we were wearing a shirt from the previous day, which they declared was unhygienic and against the rules. I didn't mind as it was hot and sticky under the roof and I just couldn't get to sleep for a long time. It really was all too much for me – the heat, the strange iron bed and the awful homesickness.

Monday morning started at 6.30 with 'Good Morning! Get up! Twenty minutes now of early morning sports in the park – gym shoes, shorts and T-shirts.'

This rude awakening prepared us for the raising of the Nazi flag and the songs 'Up with the flag' and 'Deutschland, Deutschland ueber alles, ueber alles in der Welt' (Germany, Germany above everything, above everything in the world). This tedious ceremony was repeated every day. Afterwards we had to hurry up and wash, dress and make our beds.

At breakfast the weak German coffee and dark bread tasted awful, but happily we were allowed to bring our own food to the table. Many other girls had also brought their own food, such as salami, ham and cakes. No wonder the Hitler girl in charge went mad in the middle of the week when she found out that some of the girls had written home to say the food there had made them sick.

Now to the bottom line, the admission test. What I remember most clearly are the questions that embarrassed me. The test started with German. We had to write a report about our life at home, in our village or town, at school and church, discussing our relationship with our teachers and priests, our hobbies, our activities in the Hitler Youth and how we felt about the German empire and the Fuehrer, Adolf Hitler. I was terrified I would be found out as I had concocted a story of half-truths and white lies.

After each subject we changed rooms. For me, a young girl from a village school, the long corridors in this big school were a complete puzzle. More than once I took the wrong direction. Thank goodness there were also other girls running through the corridors like lost sheep. The leader called us 'stupid geese.'

In the afternoon we had a difficult dictation test. I coped with that well enough, but, when it came to writing about the mouse buzzard, I got a bit shaky because I didn't even know what it was. So I just went ahead and made a story up.

The second day we were tested on mathematics, my worst subject. I almost fainted when the teacher started with $2a + 2b = (a + b) + (a + b)$ and $x+y = z$. She called it algebra but it was Greek to me. Only the girls from the lower high school understood it. Fortunately there were other girls in my position and we were put in a special group and given a test based on basic knowledge and geometry, enabling us to pick up a few marks.

In the afternoon it was sport and physical education in the hot July sun on the lawns by the school. Most of the girls were excited about it, but not me. It was the usual Hitler Youth 'bosh,' as my village teacher used to call it, but here in the training school they considered it highly important.

The long and high jumping, relay races, tug-of-war, leapfrog races and shotput were fiercely competitive and the teams were given names such as Tigers, Lions, Eagles, Falcons and Panthers. I can still see myself, a left-hander, trying in vain to throw a ball full swing with my right hand. The ball flew behind me three times in a row. During the long jump I made a fool of myself and landed on my bottom and in the high jump I knocked the bar off. I had let my team down and felt a complete idiot. Close to tears with all this German stupidity, I was really scared I would fail my overall tests because of my humiliating performance on the sports field.

I made up for it next day, however, in geography, when we had to draw a map of Germany with three rivers, mountains and towns, and in natural history, when we had to draw a bee and a primrose and give a detailed explanation of them both. I had learned all about these subjects, as well as physics, in which I also did well, from the heavy book I had to carry round in my bag.

They made it clear that one of the really important subjects was history, a subject they just loved to brag about. We had to know all the heroes of the German empire that Hitler said was going to last for a thousand years. Every day we were read reports of the movements of the German army, which we had to follow with pins on a wall map. We were also told how many tons of shipping the Germans were sending to the bottom of the North Sea and how they were winning the war in France, even though we all knew the Americans were pushing them back more and more each day towards their own country.

Then one day we were given a test consisting of a series of different geometrical figures and instructed to cross off the figure in each series that did not belong to the same class as the rest. I did not realize at the time that it was an intelligence test of the type in common use everywhere today.

Afterwards each of us had to go separately to see the director in person and explain in High German why we wanted to be a teacher. I was terribly nervous but found to my great relief that he was a kind man and put me completely at ease.

One of the last afternoons was reserved for painting and singing. I coped with painting, finding I could just about manage a vase of flowers but, when it came to the music lessons, I couldn't even read a note – unlike many of the girls, who had been to the conservatory of music and could even play the piano. But fortunately I have a good singing voice and was able to make up a few points there.

On the last afternoon we had to take part in a propaganda parade, marching in our gym outfits – black shorts, white T-shirts, white socks and gym shoes – through the streets of Walferdange. We looked like Hitler Youth girls as we kept in step behind our leaders while lustily singing German songs. When we arrived on top of the hill I was completely exhausted, but then we split into groups and went off to the forests to rehearse a play for the final evening. That was fun. Steffi played the piano and sang a lovely song. It rounded off the evening beautifully and was about the only part of the day I enjoyed

At last the long week of tests was over and I was exhausted. But not just from the strain of the exams, the drilling and the sports – there was another reason.

Our sleep had been broken almost every night of the week by the air-raid siren, which was located on the roof, directly above our heads. Every time it started howling we all had to tumble quickly out of bed and find our way half asleep down the stairs in a total blackout, guided only by the beam of a small flashlight, into the castle cellar, where we sat along the wall in on wooden benches, wrapped in our bed blankets. It was pretty miserable.

Outside we could hear the roaring of "the British" (that's what we used to call all the allied aircraft) flying over our heads. I wasn't worried, but some of the girls from the city and the industrialized south of the country had already been bombed and were frightened to death. Some even cried.

All in all, the raids were an extra stress-factor in a week of stress. The siren usually went off in the early hours of the morning, between one-thirty and three, rudely awaking us from the period of our deepest sleep. We all sighed with relief when we heard the all-clear and dragged ourselves gratefully back up the stairs and into our beds. The next day the program would start half an hour later.

We were told the results of the tests on Saturday morning in the great hall. Many of the girls who had been so cocky at the beginning of the week were much quieter now. But some of them, especially those who were pro-German, were still cocksure of themselves. I had no feelings either way. The Germanization of everything had almost broken my spirit and I felt very low.

Nevertheless, when my name was called out and I was told I had passed I felt a great rush of relief. But when my mother came to pick me up I couldn't hold my feelings back any longer and burst into tears.

To be back home was paradise regained. But I was a wreck and, as we say in Luxembourg, I couldn't have jumped over a straw. I had no appetite and everyone in the village commented on how skinny I was. It was simply a reaction against the teaching school and everything it stood for. As soon as the summer holidays came I speedily recovered and the memories of that awful week passed away like a bad dream.

And a bad dream it remained, thank God, for I didn't have to return to that nightmare of a school any more. In September of that year the Americans liberated us at last from our Nazi oppressors.

21 A CLOSE BRUSH WITH DEATH

IT WAS SEPTEMBER 1944 and the entire country was on tenterhooks awaiting the arrival of the American liberating armies. We knew they were close. Some said in Belgium and some France. Rumor was rife and tension was high. However, I had other things on my mind at that time. My suitcases were packed and I was ready to enroll in the teacher training school at Walferdange, on the outskirts of Luxembourg City. But little did I know what trouble lay ahead.

The entire country was living in hope of a speedy liberation, but at the same time the thought of the coming offensive on our soil weighed heavily on most people's minds. They knew they could be facing a future of terror and evacuation and feared for their homes and their land.

This fear led to all sorts of irrational behavior. People started to hide their most precious possessions in odd places, such as underground cellars and bails of hay in the barns.

My own family packed our hand-woven linen in a wooden box and built it into a cellar wall in the teacher's house. The door to the room where my father used to smoke the ham was barricaded to preserve our last reserves of ham, bacon and salami, and I helped dig a hole in the garden where we buried our wine and schnapps. We were like squirrels stocking up for the winter.

Easy to laugh about these days, but in those apocalyptic times – well, it seemed like the end of the world to us at the time – we were like drowning people clutching at straws.

Waiting for liberation was almost unbearable. A news embargo had been imposed on Luxembourg and nobody knew what was happening. Rumor reigned supreme. One minute we heard the Americans were only 20 miles away, in Arlon, just over the border in Belgium, and then we were told they were 30 miles away, near the towns of Athus and Longwy, in France. We just didn't know what to believe.

What we did know, however, was that the Germans were in full retreat. Along the main Luxembourg to Trier railway line, past our house, unscheduled trains continually thundered by, two at a time, side by side and packed with troops - and all hurtling at breakneck speed towards Germany.

Ordinary soldiers drove the engines. Without signals they raced through or crashed over rail level crossings, whether they were open or closed. Many of the freight trains were also loaded with goods looted from occupied France.

Although Luxembourgers were overjoyed to see this great unbeatable army in flight, it was sad to see the hospital trains, with sick and unhappy faces staring out of the windows.
It was even sadder as the situation worsened, when the Germans no longer used hospital trains but heaped the crippled and wounded together on the floors of cattle trucks. Against that cargo of misery, the slogan on the outside of those cattle trucks — 'Wheels must roll for victory' – struck a hollow note. We noticed with grim satisfaction that no more trains were coming from Germany, but that made it difficult and dangerous for Luxembourgers conscripted into forced labor in Germany and now trying desperately to return. They had to creep back along the tracks as best they could, keeping out of sight at all costs in case they were caught by the Germans and shot as deserters.

My own father was one of those 'deserters.' One night he slipped away with a friend during the confusion of an air raid on Ehrang and Trier, which they had escaped by the skin of their teeth. When he reached home he was tired and hungry, but a very happy man.

We kept his presence to ourselves and nobody in the village knew he was home. It would have been too risky to let anyone know. To be on the safe side my father decided to take sick leave and notify his boss in Germany. I was to cycle to the family doctor's in Grevenmacher and ask him for two medical certificates, one for me (to excuse me from going to the teacher-training school) and the other for my father.

All a waste of time really, I thought, because liberation was close and before long we wouldn't be needing any excuses. But I agreed of course to go.

Right after lunch on Friday the 8th of September I jumped on my bike and left for the doctor's in Grevenmacher. I knew the road by heart and began to enjoy the ride along the country road. It was a lovely sunny autumn day, the farmers were harvesting the late hay in the meadows and birds singing in the trees. It was idyllic.

It would have been possible to forget about the war if not for the presence of some German military vehicle rumbling and roaring along the same road. They were camouflaged with all sorts of greenery so that the American planes wouldn't spot them. I remember feeling a little uneasy about that and, as it turned out, with good reason.

However, I had forgotten my fears by the time I reached Doctor Clees' surgery. He was a lovely old doctor and had no compunction in giving me the two sick notes I needed, hastily scribbling on them that my father and I had typhoid fever.

At the same time he laughed and said: 'Once more I have to feed the Germans with a juicy lie. Still, lying to the Germans is not a sin. Now hurry home and take care the Germans don't get you!'

Before I left for home, I decided to use my ration coupons to buy some bread at the bakery and some meat at the butcher's, but my luck was out. The shelves in both shops were empty. A frustrating reminder of the war I was trying to forget. Without further waste of time I headed for home.

As I walked up the steep hill leaving Grevenmacher I noticed some people pushing a cart loaded with their belongings. They looked panic-stricken. The local people, watching from the doors or windows of the roadside houses, made it perfectly clear that these unhappy people were Luxembourgish collaborators fleeing alongside the retreating Germans. The locals hooted and laughed, calling the collaborators all sorts of rude names.

But my attention went to the two little children snuggling up to their mother behind the cart. I felt so sorry for those poor little innocents. I have never forgotten that desperately sad scene.

While I was riding full speed down the other side of the hill I suddenly noticed a German plane circling above. Then an American plane came whistling through the air and disappeared behind some trees followed by the ear-shattering thunder of anti-aircraft guns. It felt as though everything was happening just above me.

I jumped off my bike in panic and hid behind a tree. The noise of planes and firing lasted no more than a couple of minutes and suddenly everything went quiet. Not a soul stirred on the road or in the fields.

Drawing: Pascal Reimen

I leapt back on my bike and took off like the wind. When I reached the next village I saw a cloud of black smoke rising above my village. My God! What had happened?

Then I saw a group of German soldiers approaching from some distance away. I went cold with fear. What if they stopped me and searched my bag, I asked myself, and found my certificates? The closer they came the more scared I was.

I pedaled furiously by as though nothing was the matter. I had almost made it when one of them grabbed my bike from the back and screamed: 'Halt, Fahrrad her!' (Stop! Give me the bike). I almost died and cried out: 'No, please, I have to get home. I have just come from the doctor. My father has typhoid fever.'

The German cursed, let go of my bike and ran off after his comrades. 'Jesus, Mary and all the Saints, what luck I have just had,' I told myself as I got back on the bike and sped off in the direction of home.

167

The cloud of black smoke still hung over the village and the smell of gunpowder filled the air. I couldn't wait to get indoors and make sure everything was all right.

My parents were relieved to see me home and well. They had crouched in the cellar during the American air attack on the German ammunition truck. The whole cargo had exploded and the truck left a blazing wreck. The crew had got out just in time and found refuge in a nearby ditch.

My school friend Marie-Josée, who always guarded her cows at that very spot, had been saved too, thanks to the German soldiers, who had made her get into the ditch with them. She had had the horrible experience of seeing the arm of one of those poor boys being torn off by a hail of bullets.

I was so overcome listening to all that awful news that I forgot all about the sick notes. When I did get round to showing my parents the certificates with Dr Clees' 'typhoid fever' diagnosis, they couldn't stop laughing. But we soon stopped when we heard another American plane circling in the sky outside. We ran into the cellar before it dived on the remaining ammunition trucks and blasted them off the road.

When it was safe to leave the cellar we looked outside and saw smoke rising from the very road I had just cycled home along. Was I pleased to be home! Just in time too. That had been a very close call.

Then a couple of German soldiers ran over the Syr bridge. We hurried inside and locked the door, looking from behind the curtains. Two village boys, Zenon and Jull, then appeared with their horse and wagon, coming down the old rural road from Trier. The two Germans stopped them and tried to steal the horse but the farm lads had other ideas and started shouting and screaming and jumping up and down.

The horse panicked, bucked and almost knocked one of the Germans flying before running off towards the hedge. With that the Germans gave up and continued on their way up the hill. Zenon and Jull had had a lucky escape. Other Germans would have possibly killed them.

My father wanted to go outside and watch, but my mother begged him to stay with us. Suddenly a German sneaked by our house, went into the laundry room and came out pushing father's bike, jumped on it and raced off alongside the railway line towards the next village, obviously on his way to Germany. Dad ran out shouting, but it was far too late.

Then another soldier shot by on our neighbor's bike, going like the wind in the track of the first one and also in the direction of Germany. My mother then dragged my father inside while I ran to lock the laundry-house door to keep my own bike safe. For the rest of the day none of us put our noses outside.

The next day, Saturday the 9th of September, was quiet, but the Americans made up for it the day after, when their planes swooped down on the village to strafe everything German in sight.

The first we knew about it was during Sunday mass at Olingen, when we thought the world was about to come to an end. People ran screaming out of church and back into their homes. I remember us children sitting scared as rabbits under the rood screen in the back of an almost empty church while the priest continued with his service as though nothing had happened.

More attacks by American reconnaissance aircraft followed when we were at home in the afternoon. Every time we heard the rat-a-tat-tat of machine-gun fire, we ran and hid in the cellar. My brother cried and trembled like a leaf. My mother prayed and we all believed our last hour had come. By the time the day had dragged to a close we all fell into a fitful sleep, grateful to have survived.

But then on the 12th of September a great wave of excitement passed through Olingen. People started rushing from house to house, all with the wonderful news that the Americans had arrived!

Within minutes, flags in the red, white and blue of Luxembourg were fluttering from the doors of every house and even on the church steeple. Everyone seemed to be running. Someone had seen American tanks on the main road. At that moment a great crowd of villagers suddenly surged over the Syr bridge shouting and crying 'The Americans are coming!.' They poured on past us up the steep road to the main road at Banzelt, where we all joyfully joined them.

From the end of the village we could see right down the national road leading to Grevenmacher and the German border – and then, all of a sudden, God be praised, there they were! The Americans! They had finally arrived. The hour of liberation was at hand.

At the top of the road, near a pine forest, we met a jeep full of Americans coming our way. We cheered and cheered and ran laughing towards them. But the soldiers looked nervous, holding their machine guns at the ready, and didn't react to the warmth of our greeting.

We were taken aback at first as we hadn't expected that. We then ran on to the main road crossing, where the people from Flaxweiler, the next village, came pouring in to join the celebrations as more and more Americans came, their large tanks rolling over our national roads.

We screamed and waved at them regardless of their reaction, and kept up a continuous barrage of applause. Our hearts were overflowing with joy and our eyes full of tears. Then the tanks stopped on an order from one of the officers, who had a radio in his jeep. In a moment the tanks were stormed by the Luxembourg people, and the soldiers opened their hatches and stuck their heads out.

We cheered and cheered and cheered them, showering them with our flowers, and local musician Waltz Nic played a special salute for them on his saxophone. Then he played the Luxembourg national anthem, the 'Heemecht,' and we all sang along together, a ringing chorus of joy and thanksgiving.

The happiness we experienced that day with our American heroes is something I shall never forget. That glorious hour of our liberation is a priceless memory that will stay with those of us who were there for the rest of our lives.

I can still see those tanks as they continued on their way to the next village of Berg and nearer to Germany. We seemed to have stayed there forever waving them by. They came in a long convoy of tanks, trucks, all sorts of jeeps and side-cars and the soldiers all looked so different from the Germans, much more friendly and easy-going and a lot more relaxed in their comfortable fatigues.

Later some of the jeeps stopped and the soldiers got out and stretched their limbs, giving us the chance to take a closer look at them. So many of those guys were really tall and some of them, especially to a young girl, very good looking.

Lots of people offered them schnapps, but all of them refused. I guess they had other things on their mind at that particular time. But they were very free with their chewing gum, much to the delight of us children. It was then that I tasted chewing gum for the first time and whenever I see a packet, even to this day, I immediately associate it with the liberation of my country from German occupation.

When we returned home to Olingen in the evening, we saw American jeeps driving round our village. What a heartening sight! We all stood there applauding them and calling out welcome greetings in Luxembourgish. We just couldn't stop.

The American presence there, in our own village, really brought home to us the fact of our country's liberation. It was a very special moment and something that none of us who experienced it will ever forget.

22 LOST IN LIMBO

NOVEMBER 1944. After the sheer joy and excitement of liberation came the anti-climax of chaos and confusion. The Germans had been driven out of our country and the war was over – well, we thought it was – but in fact the Germans still had plenty of fight left in them and they were soon to prove it . . . at the Battle of the Bulge.

But at that time we found ourselves left in a sort of backwater, wandering around like souls in limbo. Nothing was working and everything seemed to have passed us by.

The schools everywhere were being used as lodgings for American soldiers. The German replacement teachers had fled for their lives and the Luxembourg teachers, many of whom had been deported to teach in Germany, were still working in captivity in Germany. In short, no one knew what was going on - it was all a total mess.

In Olingen our schoolteacher tried to teach the local children for a couple of hours every morning in the best living-room of the Schottesch farm, but I wasn't among them as I had already finished primary school. The school I had been admitted to in June after passing my entrance examination, the Hitler teachers' training school (the Lehrerinnenbildungsanstalt), no longer existed. Where was I supposed to go to school and, more to the point, which type of school? I had a problem.

As I wanted to be a teacher, the Luxembourg teachers' training college, the 'Fieldgen,' was the obvious choice, but it was difficult to find out what was happening in the city schools. No passenger trains were running, the telephone and postal systems weren't working and no one could leave the village without a passport issued by the American military police.

Then our local priest, Father Wiltzius, came to the rescue. He suggested we should go to Luxembourg City by bike, each on our own separate bike, riding side by side. He then obtained a pass for this trip from the local mayor and an American military police officer and we were on our way.

It was a gray foggy November day when we set off, round about noon. It was a 25-kilometre ride to the city, along the route we usually took for our annual pilgrimage. We passed the first American checkpoint at the end of our village and then through the next village, Roodt, without incident, but when we reached the main road from Luxembourg to the German border at Grevenmacher we suddenly found ourselves riding along with an army on the move.

One US convoy after another, made up of jeeps and trucks, packed full of noisy and triumphant troopers, thundered by. It was almost impossible to stay on the bikes, so wherever it was especially dangerous we dismounted and walked gingerly along the edge of the road beside the mass of military hardware rumbling by.

We kept going until to our great relief we came across the bumpy old Senningerberg pathway we had been looking for. Once on that we were safe from the traffic for some time until we reached the top of a very steep hill, where we had to rejoin all that heavy military traffic.

When we reached the nearby golf course we were stopped by a military policeman, who checked our identity cards with great care. But Father Wiltzius could manage pretty well in English and the MP soon waved us on. We went through the same routine by the airport a little further on and yet again at the 'gateway' suburb to the city, Neudorf, where the soldiers cheerfully laughed us on our way. Well, a young priest in his long flowing clergy robes and an adolescent girl, riding their bikes together – I imagine it was something quite outside their experience.

I honestly don't remember the last part of our journey, but when we managed to find the 'Fieldgen' boarding school I well remember how I was overawed by the place. It looked just like an army barracks. The school-yard was packed with jeeps and trucks and the building was buzzing with GIs.

Father Wiltzius and I waited for some time in a calm and peaceful room that offered welcome refuge from the bedlam outside. At last a nun arrived. She was the 'good mother,' as the director of a boarding school was known in those days.

I was afraid. It was the first time I had seen a nun close up. After a short chat with Father Wiltzius about the impossible conditions in the school boarding quarters because they were obliged to billet American soldiers, the talk shifted to my parents and my primary school.

While they were talking she turned her attention to me, looking me over from head to foot. My heart was in my mouth, but I needn't have worried. Father Wiltzius said what a nice child and good student I was and all the dark clouds passed away from my troubled little mind.

Whether or not I was a 'nice child' I have no idea – though I imagine I was as naughty as any normal child – but I had passed the moral and intelligence tests and that was the deciding factor in those far-off days.

Then the director called in the nun responsible for teaching the high-school grade, and I shall always remember her. She immediately put me at my ease, recognizing me right away for what I was, no more than a scared little girl from the country.

She talked about two books I needed, entitled Mortreux (for arithmetic) and Tresch (for French grammar), but which were not available from any bookshops and would have to be obtained from former students. When she heard that I had already had a French tutor, she said I might well be able to skip the first grade and start right away on the second, which was all to the good, especially as I had lost two years' normal schooling because of the war.

The only real problem was the English language, which I had not yet been taught at school. Father Wiltzius at once offered to help me and, to my great relief, the nun immediately agreed to the arrangement.

Before we left she told us to find out when the schools were going to reopen and in the meantime to study hard, to catch up on all we had missed during the occupation. I rode home with a sense of elation. I felt as though I had passed the entrance examination already.

It was almost evening when we reached the airport on our way back. The same military policeman recognized us and waved us on. But he may as well have saved his energy.

Cycling along that road was a real problem for us. Endless convoys of tanks and tracked vehicles rumbled by all the time, frightening us half to death. Trucks with open canvas tops were packed with boisterous young American boys in their fatigues and helmets, armed to the teeth with guns and machine-guns. They screamed, waved and laughed at us. We must indeed have been a sight to see – on the first bike a priest in his long clerical gown and close behind on the second bike a young girl.

Suddenly, on a sharp bend at Senningen, a jeep driven by a foolhardy soldier shot by a fraction of an inch away from us, probably trying to scare us just for the fun of it. Father Wiltzius leapt off his bike in alarm and I ran straight into him. I clutched frantically at him, knocking him completely off his balance. Then locked together in an unexpected embrace, we tumbled over and over down the slope of the bank at the side of the road.

The soldiers bent over double holding their sides and shrieking with laughter. They obviously found it funny. Well, looking back I suppose it was, though I must say I failed to see the joke at the time.

I can't tell you how we got out of that predicament, because the shock wiped it completely out of my mind. I simply cannot remember, even to this day. We thought it was a miracle that we had survived. The fright stayed with us for days. That I do remember. We told my parents and just about everyone in the village what had happened and they were all relieved, especially my parents, that we had managed somehow to get home safely without anything else happening to us, comic or otherwise.

The next day was a red letter day for me – I started to study English with Father Wiltzius. It was fun and I took to it like a duck to water and before long was able to exchange a few words with the American soldiers in our village. A little later, during German general Gerd von Rundstedt's last ditch counter offensive at the famous Battle of the Bulge, my English proved to be a great blessing to our family and to the Americans they had to communicate with.

In March 1945 I rode my bike once again to the city, but this time with my mother to find out when my schooling was going to start. No one asked for a pass on this trip but the journey was hardly less hazardous. Although by then the Battle of the Bulge had been won and the Germans were falling back in total retreat, the guns, ammunition and other U.S. military equipment still had to be transported to the front line along the Rhine and our roads were choked with military transport of every kind.

But it was nowhere near as bad as my nightmare trip with poor Father Wiltzius and my mother and I managed to make it there and back in good time. Without falling off our bikes and embracing each other!

The trip to the Fieldgen boarding school certainly wasn't wasted. We discovered that the third grade, which prepared students for the teachers' college, was already under way and that the second grade would be starting after Easter, but only for non-boarding students.

So that same day my mother took me to see her friends in the city, the Jacquemarts, to ask them if they could provide lodging and meals for me during my school days. Mother was confident they would agree as they owed us a few favors for the food and other provisions I had regularly taken to them during the long grim years of German occupation.

They didn't disappoint us, thank goodness. Otherwise I don't know what my mother would have done, for all the 'girls only' boarding schools were being used for billeting American forces and looking for private accommodation at that time was like searching for a needle in a haystack.

When school started my class consisted of 35 girls all between the ages of 14 and 20, and what a motley crew we were! Some came from the main city school, some of us from simple village schools like mine, many from schools where German teachers and school leaders had been in control and some had not gone to school at all for the past two years because they had refused to comply with the precondition of becoming members of the Hitler Youth.

But all of us were in the same boat and found it tough going getting back to some sort of normality after all those years during which proper teaching had been wiped out and replaced by harsh German discipline, brainwashing and ceaseless propaganda. It wasn't easy for the teachers either, teaching pupils from so many different streams and levels of education and ability. What's more, the cruel years of occupation had left its mark on them too.

23 A CHRISTMAS EVE TO REMEMBER

DEEP SNOW COVERED THE VILLAGES and fields. Thick icicles hung from the roofs and the Syr creek was almost completely frozen over. The church bells rang out solemnly, breaking the calm of the small village as they signaled the end of the Christmas Eve Mass, which had been held in the late afternoon instead of the traditional time of midnight, because of the war.

The villagers hurried homewards, cold and shivering from a chilly church but warm and deeply moved in their hearts from what they had experienced there. The church had been packed with American soldiers at prayer, giving thanks to God for having survived the fighting round Bastogne, in Belgium, where they had been engaged in the Battle of the Bulge, which was still raging at the time.

The joy of liberation wasn't the only reason the villagers had to hurry home. They were anxious about what lay ahead, for during the service the council chairman had told them he had had to agree to billet some thousand or so GIs in the village or else the village would have had to be evacuated.

No one resented playing host to the GIs, but the village had no more than 200 inhabitants and was already overcrowded with just as many Luxembourgers evacuated from the border towns along the River Moselle, where the Germans were making a desperate last stand in defense of their own territory.

Up until then Olingen had not been directly involved in the fighting. But just outside the village the Americans had positioned their heavy artillery and during the night they laid down a thunderous barrage attacking the German border positions in the direction of Echternach and the surrounding area. The inhabitants of the village were scared to death. At each roar of the guns, they shook in their beds and just couldn't fall asleep.

While the people were at church, events had been moving fast. They came out to find US jeeps barricading each street and pathway. Trucks stood in every farmyard and beside every house, shed and barn, big menacing tanks secured all the roads leading out of the village and Red Cross vans were parked in front of the public laundry house.

In the school playground a large tent had been set up to accommodate the field kitchen and even the schoolhouse had been taken over for military provisions. At the mill, fierce-looking soldiers stood on 24-hour guard over the officers' quarters, rifles in hand and looking as though they couldn't wait to use them.

American GIs seemed to be peering out of every habitable structure. Even the attics, the cellars and the haystacks had their quota. All you could hear spoken everywhere was American English. If a village girl happened to walk by, they were at her side in a flash, whistling, laughing, joking and shouting: 'Hi there, darling! Come and give me a kiss.' It was more like a Hollywood set piece than my quiet sleepy little village.

On returning home from church, my mother, brother and I – my father had stayed at home – were amazed to find five GIs installed in our living-room and three more in the small railroad guard house next door.

My mother was horrified when she saw the mess. On the kitchen stove steamed our huge laundry pot, heating up the water for the boys' bath, which they filled with water scooped up with their helmets, and their brand-new soiled underwear was thrown in a pile in front of the house, sprinkled with petrol and set on fire – to the consternation of my poor bemused father. We couldn't understand such waste after years of deprivation.

Once washed and dressed, the boys treated themselves to a dab of rose water and a dash of brilliantine to shine their hair. They whistled, joked and generally rejoiced in the feeling of being civilized men once again.

Then they introduced themselves: Master-Sergeant Bernard Bonk, Nick, George, Bob Longfellow, Delbert, Tom, John and Jack Campbell – all of them fine red-blooded young boys.

My father had already become friendly with them and somehow, with his double-Dutch English, had been able to make himself understood. On the kitchen table stood the bottle of prune schnapps and tiny brandy glasses. The boys all patted him on the shoulder and said: 'Oh, very good schnapps, Papa!' As the glasses clinked they all cheered and wished one another and every one of us a Merry Christmas.

As for me, the little girl, I gave those boys a big surprise when they discovered that I spoke some English. Not of course that I understood every word that emerged from the back of their American throats – especially the slang – but we got along pretty well.

On our kitchen table laid a great pile of boxes and cans filled with cakes, chocolates and candy they had received from home as Christmas gifts. Mmm...., we could smell Santa Claus. My brother and I couldn't believe our luck when those wonderful American guys filled our hands with all the candy, chocolate and chewing gum we could eat and said: 'Here, this is for you. Take it and eat it.' We were so happy. We hadn't seen so many sweets for donkey's years.

In the meantime night had fallen. Father brought in the petroleum lamp and placed it on the living-room table. There was no electricity anywhere in those wartime days. We lit up the Christmas tree with three or four candles – no more, as they were scarce at the time, like everything else, and we had to use them sparingly.

Our Americans ran in and out, shivering every time they came in and rushing immediately to the stove to warm themselves up. Then Bob Longfellow and Nick went to my mother and asked her to cook them a Christmas dinner with what they called 'American fries.' She didn't understand a word, of course, so I was recruited to do my job as interpreter and eventually worked out that what they wanted was what we call 'French fries.'

Well, potatoes we had plenty of, but where could we get the grease? Mother knew. She reached into her pantry and came out with her last precious pot of grease. The boys peeled the potatoes and cut them up in slices – and then proceeded to use the entire pot of grease. My mother nearly had a fit. She watched her carefully hoarded grease melting away and cried: 'What a waste!.' When I told the boys they should be more economical, they just laughed and shook their heads in amused disbelief.

Father then brought in a whole smoked ham from the smoke house. He slit it open and cut off a platter full of thin tender slices, crowning his efforts by producing a big jug of cider and some bottles of good Luxembourg Moselle wine. The boys were delighted. As soon as mother had set the table everyone eagerly sat round, except for Sergeant Bernard Bonk, who was on Christmas Eve duty guarding the level-crossing. It was a tight fit, with the four of us plus the eight GIs, but no one seemed to mind. This promised to be a very special meal.

The boys loved the American fries and our delicious Luxembourg ham but found the wine a little sour. Not enough to put them off though and it very quickly disappeared down where all the good wines go.

As time wore on they got merrier and merrier and became more and more talkative. They told us they had come from St Vith, in Belgium, and had been in the nearby village of Schuttrange for two days, doing nothing, it seemed, but collecting the addresses and photos of all the beautiful girls in the area, which they couldn't wait to show us. They also proudly showed us photos of their families and homes in America.

We just couldn't get over the huge cars they all seemed to drive over there and the wooden houses they lived in. It was all so different from anything we had ever seen in Luxembourg and opened up a whole new world and way of life for us.

After dinner and a dessert of the tiny canned plums we call 'mirabelles,' which the boys all loved, father surprised our GIs by starting the traditional Christmas carols with 'Stille Nacht, Heilige Nacht.' They then joined in with the English version, 'Silent Night, Holy Night'.

When we had finished John Campbell suddenly rose and, in a beautiful strong young voice, sang the stirring hymn 'Adeste Fidelis, Venite Adoremus' ('Come All Ye Faithful, Come Let Us Adore Him'). A hush fell over the entire company as the words and melody filled the house, the street and our hearts.

Drawing: Paula Antunes

And so it continued, with songs from both sides of the Atlantic, the Old World and the New. Then my little 10-year-old brother, Marcel, in response to our prompting, joined in with his wonderful choirboy voice. I noticed more than one GI wipe away a secret tear or two. Even Sergeant Bernard Bonk came in to listen, after he'd recognized the very same voice he'd heard in church earlier that day. Afterwards John Campbell lifted Marcel up to the ceiling and called out: 'Merry Christmas! God bless you! God bless us all!.'

When it was all over, two of the GIs crept upstairs to my brother's bed, but three of them had to make do on the cold floor in their sleeping bags. Then, to their delight, they discovered that mother had slipped in a hot water bottle and heated bricks. They were really moved and called out: 'Thank you, good Mama. Thank you. We'll never forget.'

Neither did they. John Campbell told us so when he came back to stay with us in September 1984 to celebrate the 40th anniversary of our country's liberation by the American forces. We've never forgotten them either. Christmas 1944 has a place of honor in our family history . . . as well as in theirs. Silent Night, Holy Night.

24 LUXEMBOURG GAMBLING LESSONS FOR GIs

FROM CHRISTMAS EVE 1944 to mid-February 1945, our home at the rail level crossing, just like other houses in Olingen, was also home to American soldiers. Five of them slept in my brother's room while three more lived close by in the railway service lodge. People today can hardly imagine what it was like to have soldiers billeted on you in those turbulent times. It was of course our duty as they were American soldiers, on our side and out there fighting for us, but the other side of the coin was the mess they made of our homes and the damage they caused

Their great kit-bags, gaiter boots, helmets, mess tins and ration boxes were always lying scattered all around. The coat stand was overloaded with fur-lined and quilted vests and damp overcoats. Each soldier always kept his rifle, cartridge belt and ammunition in the same place – on the left- and right-hand sides of the oak-wood cupboard – and none of us was allowed to touch that dangerous stuff.

No need to say how upset mom would get when the boys stormed into the house with their boots full of dirt, snow and ice and repeatedly forgot to close the door behind them. Nevertheless, she put up with all this chaos and disorder, for those tough young guys were all so far away from home and risking their lives for us. They were 'our boys' and they were all so good-hearted. We simply adopted Bob, John, Nick, Bernard and them all as family members and made them feel at home.

For their part they showed their appreciation of our hospitality and were only too eager to share their rations with us. My brother and I received plenty of chocolate, 'Hershey' bars, candies and chewing gum, mom was kept fully supplied with soap and coffee and dad could have opened a shop with all the packets of 'Lucky Strikes.' 'Camels' and 'Phillip Morris' he was given.

It was bitterly cold outside that winter of 1944-45, but inside our warm and cozy home the fires were always blazing merrily away. Dad kept the house nice and warm by keeping five fires going all over the house. Loads of coal were emptied into the cast-iron oven in my bedroom and our living-room, while the stoves in the washhouse and the railway service hut were constantly fuelled with charcoal. The cooking oven in the kitchen was fed with wood and egg-shaped briquettes and raised to a glowing heat.

Dad had to get up very early to clean the stoves and kindle the fires and, in doing so, he woke up our GIs, who immediately jumped up out of their beds, bedrolls and sleeping bags and clattered up and down the staircase. As they passed through my bedroom with their flashlights, I always hid my head underneath the blanket and pretended nobody was sleeping in my bed.

In the kitchen dad was greeted by the boys with 'Hi, Papa! Good Morning, how are you?' In return dad served them a glass of our strong homemade plum brandy, Quetsch, to keep their souls and bodies together on their way to the field kitchen outside in the freezing cold.

Once the boys were safely out of the way, my brother and I got up and hurried down to wash ourselves at the kitchen sink. We then shot off to the parish church for the morning service. Outside it was still half-dark and rather spooky as we passed groups of GIs stumbling out of the nearby barns and sheds. From the lower village — from the Knaepges house onwards — came the strong mouth-watering smell of fried eggs and bacon on the icy morning air, carried all the way from the field kitchen set up in the school playground in the middle of the village. Once there we could hardly move through the swarming crowd of soldiers.

Some of the guys were standing around chatting loudly while others were busy gulping down their American breakfast. Close by, business was already booming in two village cafés, which were really raking in the dollars.

Many soldiers assembled in the village church for Holy Mass. Among them was Bernard Bonk, our boys' staff sergeant. In the evening he told me how much he appreciated our choir's singing of the Christmas carols and the priest's sermon in English, given especially for the American soldiers.

Each day, around nine in the morning, the GIs would fall in at various village locations. On this particular day, jeeps, trucks, radio cars and ambulances were waiting to leave, their engines running, making an infernal noise and polluting the fine clear cold morning air with their foul exhaust fumes.

Finally all the officers, from lieutenants to colonels, arrived. They gave discreet orders to the soldiers, who wrapped up in their coats, loaded up all their military gear and baggage and climbed on to their trucks. We felt desperately sorry for those poor boys, off to defend our country against Von Rundstedt's battle-hardened army, throwing everything into a last-ditch desperation counter-attack.

Our local youngsters stood around looking on, their hands tucked into their warm pockets. Some of them were eager to know where the battalion was moving off to, but of course they were wasting their time. It was all hush-hush and top-secret.

Once the convoy had finally left, all the shepherd dogs stopped their incessant barking and our quiet little farming village, nestling peacefully along the Syr creek beside the Luxembourg-Wasserbillig-Trier railway, was restored to its usual calm. The sub-zero temperature somehow seemed to accentuate the lifelessness of the streets, gardens and fields. Every now and then an American jeep or truck would pass through on patrol, the only sign of military activity to be observed during those grim days when the Battle of the Bulge was raging in the north of our country.

We wouldn't have had any idea how the battle was going if we hadn't got the miller's radio to keep us up to date with the news. No one was allowed to leave or enter the village and the mill was the only place supplied with electricity at that time.

All the roads and pathways out of the village were blocked by US tanks. Behind our own house, for instance, a big Sherman tank had taken up position. My brother and his comrades had managed to make friends with the tank crew, who allowed them to crawl around and play inside the fighting compartment of the lethal steel monster. One day I went along to see them and find out what they were doing, only for a short time, but my mother was furious and called me back at once. This type of adventure wasn't for her daughter! Aggrieved and resentful, I had nonetheless to scuttle back to my English grammar and vocabulary studies.

Meanwhile mom was busy clearing and cleaning the house. She couldn't help feeling a bit upset when she noticed the damage the boys had done everywhere in the house, especially to our furniture. She decided to lock up all her personal items, everything the boys didn't need, rolled up the carpets, draped the sofa with sheets and the dining-table with waxed cloth, took the best chairs up to the bedroom and replaced them with the kitchen chairs and the garden bench.

It may have seemed unkind, but it was the only way for us local people to protect our property. It was widely known that the houses where American soldiers were billeted got pretty rough treatment. Admittedly, the damage may have been peanuts compared with the real devastation suffered by civilians caught up in the fighting, but that was no reason to avoid it if we could.

When our boys returned home in the evening they didn't notice a thing. For them it was still the same warm, cozy and welcoming house they had been living in since they arrived in Olingen. As was so often the case, they were stiffened by the intense cold and threw their dirty boots in the corner and stretched their half-frozen feet along the warm stove. Then dad appeared with a bottle of brandy and gave the boys a shot or two of their favorite drink to warm them up. Mom soon followed on with a pot of steaming coffee to really restore their spirits and put them in the best of humor.

As was customary every evening, Mr. Bernard Bonk, as we respectfully addressed the staff sergeant, installed himself at the table near the petroleum lamp, where he put a portrait of his beautiful young wife, Dorothy, and started writing a long letter to her. They had just married the previous May, the day after Bernard had got drafted, and his men respected this daily writing ritual and left him alone with his thoughts.

They drifted off to the washing house, where dad had heated a big kettle of water. Then they washed their bodies and scrubbed themselves to their hearts' delight. While they were sprucing themselves up, we had supper in the kitchen. Afterwards, smelling like roses, those perfumed guys came wafting into the dining-room to join us for the traditional winter evening family gathering.

Dad brought in the playing cards, showed them to the boys and wrote '66' on a railway stationery pad. In mixed language consisting of Luxembourgish, German and English, he explained solemnly that '66' is the name of the card 'spiel' (game). 'You spiel (play) with me,' he said. I was then called in as his interpreter and gave a few explanations. The boys understood and all screamed together: 'OK, Papa 66. Let's go!' Dad shuffled the cards and dealt. Right away those guys knew what they were doing and held the cards the right way or 'comme il faut,' as dad said, in their hands.

The game started without more ado. Dad played 'Hearts 10' on the table and told Bob to carry on. 'It's your turn.' 'Which card, Papa?' 'Egal' (anyway you like), dad replied and stuck up his thumb, meaning one. Then Nick and John each threw a card on the table. Dad added up the value of the cards, noted it on a writing pad and heaped the cards together onto his pile, because it was he who had originated the game. He had to explain this maneuver, which he managed to do by gesturing with his fingers. Then the boys learned that the 'King' equaled four points and the 'Dame' or 'Queen' was worth only three points.

In the meantime dad had to get to know the English names of the cards. The 'As' became 'Ace' and the card we call a 'Bauer' (farmer) became a 'Jack.' What a coincidence! Dad's name was Jack. We exploded with laughter, while poor dad looked perplexed. He thought the joke was that his name was somehow related to 66. Anyway, he kept smiling and drew a big zero for Jack's value on the pad. 'OK, Jack is nuts!' yelled one of the boys. 'Nuts! What's that?' asked dad. 'Nuts means zero,' came the reply.

At once I lifted our cat from my knees, stepped over to the table and stood behind my father and wondered how 'nuts' could mean 'zero.' That was new to me. Thereupon dad asked me to help him by explaining the game to the boys, which is precisely what they wanted me to do. I accepted with many misgivings. Interpreting is never an easy job and I had only recently started learning English. What's more, we didn't even have a dictionary in the house.

Well, I did my best, but came across many words and expressions I didn't know. But dad wouldn't give up. He pronounced 'on' for 'one,' 'fiff' for 'five,' 'tunty' for 'twenty' and so on. But the boys managed to understand him and somehow or the other they all got by. And dad too, for his part, picked up a lot of words from them – to general amusement and lots of laughter.

The cards flew more and more fluently round the table. Bob and John became pretty smart gamblers while Nick was already pulling off trick after trick. Dad knocked on the table, laughing and joking, and the correct cards emerged as though by magic at the right moment. The boys made great progress and often surprised dad, who really had to struggle to win some rounds. A lot of the fun degenerated into friendly chaos but at the end of the evening everyone ended up having a really good time.

About nine o'clock the US artillery on the hillside at the edge of the village opened up and started shelling the German border. We trembled a bit at first but after a while we began to get used to it. Our GIs couldn't care less. In fact they hardly seemed to notice it. They calmly continued gambling – and so did dad.

Suddenly, during a moment of high spirits, the living-room door was flung open by Bernard Bonk, who shouted out: 'Chicago!' a secret code word. As though the devil himself was behind them, our boys leapt up, dropped all their cards and dashed for their rifles, put on their helmets, grabbed their coats and ammunition boxes and in a flash of an eye were gone from the house and out into the night.

Drawing: Silvio Marques

We were scared. We listened to the night. Apart from the hollow noise of the artillery, we couldn't hear a sound. None of us dared to step outside. After a while the boys came back smiling, heaped their weapons and equipment in their respective corners and returned to their seats round the table. Dad filled the glasses with cider and the boys gave him a resounding cheer. 'OK, Papa, let's go! One more 66!'

In fact nothing had happened outside the house or along the railway. The staff sergeant was merely testing his men. It was a mock exercise and the boys had come out of it with flying colors.

It is truly miraculous how peacefully and enjoyably we lived together with our GI guests in our small but comfy house at the Olingen level crossing while the fearsome Battle of the Bulge was being fought to its bloody finish not so very many miles away. We were fortunate to remain unharmed in those dangerous times, let alone being able to look back on it with gratitude for the brief happiness we found there in the company of our young American liberators.

25 NEW YEAR'S EVE AND A SAD GOODBYE

1944, THE YEAR OF OUR LIBERATION, ended with deep snow and thick ice and the Battle of the Bulge was raging on our borders. That New Year's Eve, the American soldiers who had been billeted on us for the past week returned exhausted to the shelter of our home from the secret military operations behind enemy lines they had been engaged in every day since they had arrived.

It was dark. They looked worn out and were not cheerfully casual as usual. They put their helmets, rifles and ammunition in the corner and hung their uniforms on the coat rack. No talking, no joking! Some went straight to mother's laundry house while others gathered round our kitchen sink to wash up. Their deathly silence was strange. Something must have happened that day. Even dad's much vaunted schnapps failed to snap them out of it.
At last Nick blurted out: 'We had a terrible time today.' That was all we could get out of him. Anxiously we wondered what had happened to them.

Staff Sergeant Bonk installed himself at the table near the oil lamp and, as usual, wrote to his wife. While he was quickly writing page after page, I could see him wipe his eyes and blow his nose several times. Jack was sitting on the sofa, leafing through a prayer book. Nick was reading Life magazine but remained uncharacteristically quiet too. He wasn't even cracking jokes about the sexy pin-ups. Very odd.

In the railway hut, where five of our boys generally had lots of fun, silence reigned. Only Bob Longfellow left the hut and nervously entered the house. He wrenched open the door and the latch came off in his hand. He swore softly. But Dad soon found a pair of pliers, a hammer and a screwdriver and fixed it, Bob helping him. Bob went back to the hut and soon returned with a packet of Lucky Strikes, which he gave my father.

In the meantime mother brought two apple pies to the table. She had baked them in the afternoon when the boys were out of the house and not around to bother her. She also brought out a bowl of the finest pudding cream. By tradition, New Year's Eve was to be celebrated in fine style. Nevertheless, the guys failed to react. Mom offered a slice of pie to each of them but they all declined with a quiet but firm 'No thank you, Mom.' They all looked so depressed. We just didn't recognize them as the happy-go-lucky boys we knew before. Eventually no one moved around and we all stopped talking to one another.

Finally I plucked up courage and told Nick I now knew that the animal they were intending to hunt in the woods was called a 'deer' in English and not a horse, as I had told them the previous evening. The misunderstanding had arisen when George and Delbert heard that our neighbor the miller had been out hunting with some of the soldiers billeted with him and that they had killed a deer (I had seen the miller's wife pickling the best chunks of deer meat), so our two GIs wanted to have a go too.

They had asked dad all sorts of questions about the woods next to our house and of course I had to play the role of interpreter. But I didn't know all the right words, so I made sketches of rabbits and hares on my drawing pad. The boys then made a few sketches, but of an animal similar to a horse. At once I said: 'Yes, that's it. There are many horses living in the forest.' 'Horses?' they asked, incredulously. 'Yes, yes,' I replied. 'Horses.' They looked at each other, shook their heads and burst out laughing.

I knew I had made a fool of myself and my stupid drawing only made them laugh all the more. If only I had had a dictionary! Then Jack, trying to help me, drew a wagon behind the animal. That did it. My confusion was complete. I felt my face turn bright red and the GIs laughed their heads off.

The next day, when I went to our parish priest, Father Wiltzius, for a private English lesson, he told me the word I needed was 'deer.' Then it was my turn to laugh, even though it was at myself, for I could see the funny side of it. So could the priest. So much for my few brief weeks of English lessons!

Anyway, I decided to tell the whole story to Nick on that solemn New Year's Eve to try to cheer up the boys and give them a laugh. Bernard listened, George smiled, Jack looked up and put his prayer book on one side, while Delbert rushed out of the house and into the hut. A moment later all the boys were gathered round me, smiling all over their faces and joking about horses and deer and deer and horses. It had worked!

In no time at all they all seemed to have forgotten whatever was troubling them and very soon they were all chatting happily away and enjoying a good laugh. The next stage in the recovery of their good humor was the rapid disappearance of mother's delicious pie and cream pudding.

Then it all began to seep out. Bob started telling us about the awful time they had had that dreadful day. Somewhere along the German border they were attacked by the Germans. During the skirmish some of their own guys got badly wounded, four of them being blown apart by German shells. Tears were running down Nick's cheeks. Bernard left the room and all the others looked down on the floor.

George took a little chain with a cross and medallion out of his pocket and showed it to us. It had belonged to his friend who had been killed. He told us he would send it to the boy's mother back home in America. Then Jack showed us a prayer book and some photographs of a friend of his who had also been killed in the very same attack.

I shuddered. My parents couldn't hide their tears. None of us said a word. We all felt overcome by the misery of the war. Thank God our eight soldiers had escaped unharmed.

Finally my father rose from his chair, wiped his eyes and took out the playing cards from the cupboard. 'Come on, boys,' he said. 'Let's gamble a sixty-six.' That cheered them up. 'OK, Pop,' they said. 'Let's go.' They all sat round the table, and the game started. It was a good game, but quieter than usual, much quieter, that evening.

In the meantime I found myself admiring the photographs of the young man who had been killed. He looked so happy among his family in front of their wooden home somewhere in Minnesota, the state where my mother's two sisters Josephine and Mary lived. The prayer book lay on the sofa but I dare not touch it. It was already late and I had to go to bed. I felt so sad it took me ages to fall asleep.

At midnight I awoke suddenly to the roar of American artillery, thundering away on the outskirts of the village. The Americans were sending their 'New Year greetings' to the Germans dug in along the banks of the Sauer river around the city of Echternach, their last line of defense. From the living-room under my bedroom I could hear our boys shouting: 'Happy New Year, Mama! Happy New Year, Papa!' I heard the glasses clinking and dad responding by cheering along with Nick, Jack, Bob, George, Delbert, John and Jim. Bernard Bonk must have come in from guard duty because I heard the boys and dad greeting him too. 'Happy New Year! Happy New Year!'on and on it went, accompanied by the thundering of the artillery, which must have gone on for at least half an hour.

Those poor Germans. What a start to the New Year for them! But what an exciting welcome to the New Year it was for us Olingen Luxembourgers! We'd never known anything like it before in our whole lives.

Eventually my parents went off to bed and the GIs tucked down inside in their sleeping bags, but I don't believe anyone had a good night's sleep that night after all that excitement. It was a short night too, for the boys were up bright and early on New Year's morning. When they returned from their breakfast in the schoolhouse playground, they brought back a whole heap of new rations. They gave stacks of cigarettes to dad and bars of soap and canned corned beef to mom. As for me, I got lots of New Year kisses and more chocolate, chewing gum and candies than I had seen for years. Not all to myself, of course, as half were for Marcel.

As it was a Sunday, my father and I were getting ready to go to church when a US jeep drove past the gate and stopped near our house. An officer jumped out and asked for the 'little railway girl who speaks English.' That was me! The officer needed me as interpreter for people in the village. I felt OK about it as it was not the first time I had been asked to do that job. So, instead of going to church, I climbed into the jeep and went with the officer and his driver to all the houses that had been vacated by US soldiers that very morning and which now needed to be told that a new draft of GIs was on the way.

Mission accomplished. The officer took me straight back home, helped me out of the jeep and gave me five dollars and a military salute. I watched the jeep dash off and then rushed into the kitchen with a big smile. I felt really proud of myself.

Then all of a sudden, just after we had finished lunch, our GIs stormed into our house like an invading army. As fast as the wind, they packed their goods, clothes and other belongings into their duffle bags, put on their coats and helmets, buckled on their cartridge belts, slipped their rifles over their shoulders and made their goodbyes, before we'd had time to take it all in. 'Thank you, thank you, Mama and Papa!' they call cried in unison. Astonished and confused, we all stood around in the kitchen watching it all going on before eventually realizing that our boys had to leave. Off to the front again, pushing on into Germany. We felt both afraid for them and upset ourselves to see them go.

Drawing: Paula Antunes

My mother, my brother and I were all weeping. Dad brought out a bottle of Quetsch, their favorite brandy, but the boys hadn't got time to drink it. Duty called and they had to go.

Staff Sergeant Bernard Bonk was upset too, but for quite a different reason. Two of his men, Nick and George, were missing. But it proved to be nothing to worry about. They hadn't gone absent without leave or anything like that. We learned later that they had only gone to Luxembourg City to a Protestant church service. Then just before they left, Bernard Bonk gave mom an envelope and asked her not to open it until they had gone.

In a matter of minutes the house was empty. Well, that's how it felt. 'Our boys' were gone. Slowly mom opened the envelope. Inside were eight dollars, with a slip of paper with the names of the eight American soldiers who, from Christmas Eve 1944 to New Year's Day 1945, had found a warm and cozy home with us. We were all deeply moved. We had spent so many happy hours with those lovely boys during the short time God had blessed us with their presence. They had brought so much warmth and love into our lives during those sad, bleak and wintry days of the Battle of the Bulge.

26 THE LONG SLOW ROAD TO RECOVERY

IT TOOK MORE THAN THE LIBERATION of Luxembourg for life to return to normal for most people in the country. In fact the hardship we had had to endure under Nazi rule certainly didn't disappear overnight. Merchandise may well have been no longer subject to rationing, but a fat lot of good that did us when there was no merchandise to buy, beg or borrow in the first place. Indeed most of us still had to scrimp and save to get by, which we managed to do by living off the food, clothing and whatever else our rich liberators, the American soldiers, threw away or gave us.

Those guys wanted for nothing. Compared with the destitute German military, who had almost nothing left to eat and, in their frantic retreat, confiscated just about everything they could lay their hands on, the GIs were surely one of the most pampered armies the world has ever seen. But no one could criticize them for that. They were generous to a fault and only too eager to trade, swap, exchange and give away large parts of their rations to the Luxembourg people. Without them many of us would have been in desperate straits.

We children especially were the principal beneficiaries of their generosity. We had never seen so many sweets and packets of chewing gum in our lives. I can still remember the chocolate, tons of it mostly in the form of 'Hershey's bars' in olive-green wax cartons, and we gorged ourselves on it until we were fed up with it, demonstrating the truth of the old Luxembourg saying 'When the mice are full, the flour loses its flavor.'

But there was also another more cogent reason. This army ration chocolate had a medical use, containing a variety of vitamins designed to provide a sufficient daily emergency diet for a soldier in the field when he didn't have access to the normal field-kitchen provisions. It can well be imagined then what it did to our tiny little stomachs, many of us falling sick with diarrhoea and some even requiring medical treatment from the American army doctors.

It wasn't just the children who benefited from the generosity of the American army – everyone did, especially those living in the vicinity of the GI field kitchens. Those with a head for business soon had their homes stocked up with all sorts of military-issue canned food and goods, and 'corned beef and beans' regularly appeared on the daily menu of many a Luxembourg family.

Apart from the types of food well known to Luxembourgers, we came across many products we'd never even heard of before, such as ketchup, Nescafé, milk powder, and dehydrated powdered eggs, as well as mouth-watering canned pineapples, apricots and peaches, not forgetting that soft snowy white bread. The Americans wasted so much of it, but how we loved it! After the awful gray German bread, that lovely bread the Americans threw away was a real treat for us, especially when thickly coated with US orange or apricot jam.

Luxembourgers also made good use of the clothes and equipment stocked in the barns and sheds where the GIs were billeted and often left behind when they moved on. According to army regulations, of course, all excess military clothing and related equipment were supposed to be handed in by the soldiers, but like so much else in wartime it just didn't work out that way. Fortunately for us. Naturally our people were not slow in using their initiative and imagination here, with mothers and daughters only too eager to help the soldiers out in every way they could, cleaning out barns and sheds, sorting, washing and mending. And when the soldiers left all sorts of US clothing – underwear, shirts, sweaters, jumpers, trousers, field jackets, woolen blankets, towels and socks, etc. - suddenly began to appear on garden laundry lines.

What's more, all that US clothing was brand-new issue and top quality, as were the raincoats, leather shoes and solid gaiter boots that had so often been swapped against a liter of homemade plum or apple brandy. For years after the war Luxembourg men could be seen in town, strutting around as though on a fashion parade, proudly displaying garments once worn by American soldiers.

Toilet items too were much in demand, such as Colgate toothpaste, enabling Luxembourgers to once again brush and protect their teeth, and hair cream, which was particularly popular with the young males, who loved nothing better than to comb, brush and groom their hair in the up-to-date American style.

But nothing could beat cigarettes in the popularity poll in those far-off days when almost every young man seemed to smoke and no one had any idea what a dangerous and addictive habit it was. Youngsters would do anything to get hold of a load of 'Camels' or 'Lucky Strikes' and, if they really 'struck lucky,' a zip-lighter too. The young boys didn't miss out either. Each set his heart on getting his hands on a US army jack-knife, universally looked on as a prize possession.

As for us girls, we didn't do so well. Quite understandably, of course. An army of young men, were hardly likely to leave clothing and equipment calculated to excite the interest of young females. A few odd bottles of perfume here and there, were about all, some of us managed to salvage. No bottles of perfume ever came my way, but Sergeant Bonk did present me with a modern graphite pencil with a retractable graphite lead. I treasured it like a sacred relic and never thought for one moment of using it until I became a high-school student.

I never cease to be amazed too when I think of all the everyday items much sought after as valuable antiques these days that lay around discarded and ignored at that time. Today many of them would be worth a small fortune. I saw many an American helmet lying in the gutter and filled with water, with cats and dogs drinking from them. Small children played regularly in the sand with soldiers' mess tins, knives, forks and spoons that could be folded over. Those that are left are now on display in war museums.

As for the farmers, the good times rolled for them. They were able to buy US jeeps for as little as an apple and a slice of bread, not to mention rolls of barbed wire to fence in their cattle, tent tarpaulin and solid canvas to cover piles of straw – all at knock-down prices or even nothing at all.

You could hardly pass a house in those days without seeing shiny bright shell cases standing proudly on the windowsills. Those shell cases lay in profusion around the American artillery emplacements, where they had been discarded, and were therefore easy to acquire. It was all the rage at the time to engrave or stamp the Luxembourg Red Lion or national coat-of-arms on them, thereby turning them into works of art. These days they are in great demand everywhere at collectors' or antiques fairs.

On the negative side was the problem of live ammunition, shells and grenades left lying around, similar to the situation in the Third World former war zones today. Many a tragic accident occurred when young people - as naturally curious in Luxembourg as anywhere else in the world - picked them up and played with them or even stumbled on them inadvertently.

I too had a nasty experience with a war relic and could well have lost my life as a result. Although it didn't explode, which usually happened, it proved to be equally dangerous in quite another and totally unexpected way.

One day near the Syr creek bridge, my brother and his friend Emil, the miller's nephew, discovered something that looked like a small boat and they took it to the mill on a small handbarrow. The miller, whom we called Uncle Joss and who was there at the time, told them it was one of the spare fuel tanks used as additional fuel containers for German fighter aircraft.

The miller then had the brilliant idea of fixing a US jerry can to each side of the empty fuel tank to balance it in the water and make a 'boat' for the two boys to use on the mill pond. Suitable paddles were soon produced and in the wink of an eye Marcel and Emil were having the time of their lives splashing across the pond in their exciting new 'boat.'

News of Uncle Joss's invention spread like wildfire through the village and very soon the boys from the farm and Marcel's and Emil's friends turned up to take a look at this new form of water transport. To their surprise they saw Marcel and Emil venturing by then into the deep water close up to the lock. And they weren't stopping there. Slowly and proudly, before the envious eyes of their friends, they passed under the railway bridge and along the lock before heading off towards Roudemer brook.

More and more local people came along to see what has happening, among them Schouttesch Joss, shaking his head and puffing his pipe, and his brother Theophile, hurrying to the bridge in his burlap apron and shouting out in amazement.

Suddenly everyone seemed to be there at once, crowding on the bridge, some of them laughing and joking, others arguing and criticizing. Then a few more querulous voices made themselves heard. The Ziirden family in particular didn't seem at all impressed and before long Uncle Joss himself became a little concerned for the safety of the boys.

So Nic Sauber, a local mechanic, took the vessel into his workshop and made it safer by soldering the two jerry cans on to the fuel tank. Then he let his son Fernand, a friend of Marcel's and Emil's, join in the fun and their friends Will and Romain were not long in following. From then on it was 'plain sailing.' The boys went on to have a lot of fun and the watching crowd enjoyed it too. That particular chapter ended on a happy note.

A few weeks later it was Pentecost, which I spent at home on holiday from the Fieldgen High School in Luxembourg City, where I had since become a student. As I had heard all about the boat by then, I went along to the Syr creek to see how the boys were getting on. My brother then invited me to join them. Great! Well, that was my first reaction. Then I thought about it and hesitated. But Marcel insisted and eventually I gave way, despite my slight misgivings. I didn't want to seem a sissy after all. However, I soon began to enjoy myself and I was splashing and fooling about, like the rest of them, and before long I was taking the boat out by myself.

Drawing: Paula Antunes

The next day, after finishing my mathematics homework, I teamed up with Marie-Josée Ziirden on another boat trip. With increasing confidence and enthusiasm we paddled up and down the Syr creek like a couple of Olympic rowers. Our neighbor's ducks didn't seem to mind the disturbance, gliding swiftly away each time we passed, but the male duck quacked his protests loudly and disappeared disgruntled under the willows.

We were really enjoying ourselves. I then caught sight of the village church, with its short tower, reflected in the crystal-clear water. I looked up at the Syr railway bridge, the mill, the quiet village, the nearby Nures and Widdenberg forest and the entire skyline of the surroundings and felt a profound sense of peace and happiness. It was a magic moment. Almost a psychedelic experience or an epiphany.

But as usual there is no light without darkness and what followed very nearly brought a total eclipse to that joyful moment of serenity. As Marie-Josée and I rowed up the Roudemer Brook, Emil Jull caught sight of us from the bridge. We waved happily at him and continued to do so as we rowed. At that moment Marie-Josée tried to stretch her long legs and sit up higher in the boat. It was the worst thing she could have done. The boat promptly tipped over. She managed to leap off just in time and save herself but I found myself upside-down in the water, lying trapped under the boat.

I tried to call for help but my mouth immediately filled with water. I struggled frantically to free myself, but my legs remained trapped in the boat. I felt myself sinking into the mud of the creek as though being drawn down by quicksand. I could still hear the screams of bystanders echoing in my head as the thought flashed through my mind that I was going to drown.

At that moment I felt a strong hand grasp me by the shoulder and drag me out of the boat and pull me to safety on dry land. It was Emil Jull. He had saved me. I was in a state of total confusion. I couldn't stop coughing as water ran out of my mouth, my nose and my ears. My wet and dirty clothes clung to me. I was covered in slimy mud and shivering with cold that cut through me like ice. I thought I was going to die.

Marie-Josée's sisters had come and taken her home. Josef and Theophile, the neighborhood farmers, fussed over me until their niece Marie arrived and quickly took me into their house and brought me some clean dry clothes. First I had a good wash at their kitchen sink and then put on the clothes she had given me. After a cup of hot coffee I felt a lot better and half an hour later I sneaked home across the meadows. I must have looked a sight flapping along in Marie's big slippers and wearing clothes that were much too big for me. Still, I didn't care. I was safe. That's all that mattered.

As soon as I got home mum realized right away what had happened and gave me a good telling-off. I was only too relieved to get away at last into my bedroom and reflect on my miraculous escape. My God, I thought, if the accident had occurred near the lock or in the middle of the pond, we would have both been drowned. Not even brave, strong Jull could have pulled us out of the deep water there. I shuddered. God's hand was surely on us that eventful day.

I really don't remember whether or not I thanked Jull at the time, or even later. Traumatic accidents do in fact tend to black out the period that immediately follows. I put that right, however, when my book was publicly launched at Olingen and I formally acknowledged him as the man who saved my life. He was as proud as a peacock when he read what I had written. But he deserved it. I owed him my life.

27 REVIVAL OF THE ECHTERNACH DANCING PROCESSION

FOR THE INHABITANTS OF OLINGEN, the 22nd of May 1945, the Tuesday after Whit Sunday, was a day of jubilation, a great day in fact for all the people of Luxembourg. For the first time since the Liberation, the traditional and famous Dancing Procession could take place again at Echternach. Exceptionally our local band was asked to be part of the show and therefore everyone in the village wanted to accompany the fanfare.

The Dancing Procession, a religious festival, which dates back to the Middle Ages, had been banned by the Nazis, who had dissolved all the bands and confiscated the instruments. They didn't get them back either, as most of them had vanished altogether in the chaos of the widespread evacuation and destruction of the Moselle and Sauer villages during the Battle of the Bulge when the brief and abortive German counter-attack took place. Some of those instruments even ended up in America as GIs' souvenirs.

But Olingen, which escaped the evacuation of war-zone villages, had a few sharp minds that managed to outsmart the Germans and hide the instruments, the cash-coffers, the uniforms and the flag of the band when the Wehrmacht occupied the village in May 1940. On Liberation Day, September 12 in 1944, the instruments were brought out again and proudly played for the American liberators.

As the day of the procession approached Olingen found itself in the enviable position of being the only village with a fully equipped band and was consequently invited by the seminary professor, Father Donckel, to play at the Echternach Dancing Procession.

It was a proud day for Olingen and the whole village was in a state of great excitement, with the musicians busy rehearsing in their rooms all week. The haunting melody could continually be heard echoing throughout the village. You just couldn't get it out of your head. Everyone was humming it all day long. It spread like an epidemic, as catchy tunes do.

We children too were caught up in all the excitement and were going round singing something about 'Adam and his seven sons.' We were all training and telling one another how to do the dancing at the procession – three steps forward and two steps back, all the time holding on to your neighbor by a white handkerchief. It all sounded so exciting to our young minds and we just couldn't wait for the starting date. Places had to be reserved too on the transport taking us to Echternach. My father, bless him, had wasted no time, making sure we got a place too.

Finally the big day arrived. Already at six in the morning Nicky the mechanic from the local workshop 'Bertess' had his tractor, complete with a long trailer hitched on behind, parked outside the band's assembly hall. The benches and instruments were first placed on the trailer and then we all piled on, the band, the priest, the people and finally the children. It was a bit of a crush, but nobody cared. We children just sat on someone's lap or squeezed in between some adults. 'Better a bad ride than a comfortable walk,' the adults were saying.

At half past six precisely, Jull, the big drummer, sounded a roll on his drum to signal our departure. Nicki cranked his

Zettelmeyer tractor and we were off. We first passed the school, where the teacher and Mrs. Jakoby stood outside, smiling all over their faces and waving us goodbye. As we crossed the bridge and passed through the outskirts of the village we were warmly greeted by all the people who had stayed behind to look after the animals in their stables or do other necessary routine jobs. They were lining the road and laughing happily as we rumbled by.

 Spring was in the air. The war had just come to an end. Everyone was happy. Even the animals in the fields seemed to be smiling. The wind that whipped round our ears as we rolled towards Betzdorf was on the chilly side, but the sun was coming up with the bright promise of a warm spring day for the coming celebrations. Nature too was looking her best, joyfully attired in the varied shades of green of early spring. Just about everything seemed to match our light and careless mood.

In Wecker we took on two more people and then carried on, past Biwer, Boudler and many of the other villages that had been evacuated when the Germans had briefly but brutally returned during the Rundstedt Offensive. Here the picture started to take on more somber hues. All the houses were in a terrible state, as American soldiers had been billeted in them during the winter months. In one house we passed I noticed a rusty oven pipe hanging out of the window and a whole twisted coil of cables running up over the house and across the street.

In Bech a farm had been hit by a shell and burnt out, including the house and the stables. And many other houses in the vicinity had lost all their windows. Up the hill and past the Geyesch farm, we could see how fierce the offensive had been. The wood that had once stood there had been entirely destroyed by intensive shelling, with giant craters pitted everywhere and the burnt-out remains of German trucks and an American tank. Unexploded mines too lay all around and the area was ring-fenced with warning signs. Nowhere was safe. It was really scary.

Before we joined the Echternach road, we took a break. By then the women and children were ready for the sandwiches and flasks of warm coffee we had brought with us, while the men enjoyed their coffee with a traditional shot of schnapps. As we continued on our merry way, our priest started to pray to Saint Willibrord, whose burial place at Echternach was the destination of our day of pilgrimage and pleasure. While he was praying, we slipped dutifully into our pilgrim role of penitence and prayer. As a result a passing convoy of American soldiers looked at us in a mixture of amusement and incredulity.

We arrived in Echternach about 9 o'clock, already upset by the destruction we had seen. But nothing could have prepared us for the scenes of devastation we saw in Echternach. Many houses had been totally destroyed, leaving little more than piles of burnt-out rubble, and many more were damaged beyond repair, with vast gaping holes in roofs and walls. Hardly any doors or windows remained. Most of the people lived in their cellars while waiting for their homes to be rebuilt. The entire city looked deserted, almost like a ghost town.

The market square had obviously taken the brunt of the attack. It had been entirely devastated. I couldn't believe my eyes. However, the oldest listed building in Echternach, the town hall or 'Denzelt,' dating back to the 11th and 12th centuries, had miraculously escaped damage, but the famous cathedral or 'Basilika' lay in ruins, because the Germans had blown it up on Christmas Eve before they fled the city. Only the crypt, which dates back to the 7th century and contains the tomb of Saint Willibrord, escaped damage.

Drawing: Filipe Da Costa

What was all the more upsetting for us was that we knew the bombardment of the town had been directed from our own village, Olingen, where the Americans had set up their artillery to drive the Germans out of Echternach by a carpet barrage of murderous shelling.

We were told to take up our place at the Sauer-bridge or rather where the bridge used to be. What was left of it was lying in the river, another casualty of the mass destruction. As we looked in dismay at the sorry sight we began to catch the first strains of the haunting notes of the famous Echternach melody. It was still some way away, but coming ever nearer. A frisson of excitement passed through our group and we began to get restless.

Finally it was our turn and suddenly we were off. Our flag carrier Pierre Engel marched proudly on ahead. The bandleader struck the first note, the band took up their cue and almost at once they were all playing their hearts out and marching merrily along in jaunty step. The rest of us, the people of Olingen, fell in behind, doing our best to keep in step and march in time.

As we danced around the market square we were able to observe this extraordinary procession and soon began to pick up the steps and really enjoy it, even though many of us seemed to be finding it hard going. The deeply religious atmosphere of the occasion could be strongly felt, but everyone seemed to be having a marvelous time as well, which may well have had something to do with the fact that it was the first procession since the end of the war.

The procession then began to move more slowly as we started dancing up the stairs to the old church on top of the hill. I had to laugh at my father. He was in front of me and wearing a backpack, and every time he jumped the backpack jumped with him.

The procession ended on a high note - or rather an ear-shattering blast - when two bands played at the same time in the rather small church. I really thought my eardrums were about to explode. Finally we stood outside the church and sadly watched the end of the procession from the top of the hill. What made it all the more sad was a bird's-eye view we had from that viewpoint of the widespread destruction of the historic city of Echternach and the Basilika down below.

After it was all over we had a picnic on the banks of the River Sauer, which runs between Luxembourg and Germany in a region badly damaged by the fighting, especially in the town of Echternacherbrueck. During the picnic I lost my father, who had wandered off somewhere with the band, all of them in a happy and festive mood and set on having a good time. But no one was worried. They all got safely back before we left, except for two who probably had too much to drink. Comrade Nick went off to look for them and it was ages before he managed to find the two 'lost sheep' and bring them back.

On the way home we traveled on the road that runs alongside the Sauer, where once again we witnessed the terrible havoc created by the conflict. But it was even worse on the German side of the river, where hardly anything seemed to be left. Then we noticed some German farmers collecting hay and something very nasty happened.

Everyone started swearing and cursing, invoking all manner of evil upon those Germans. It was shameful behavior for Christians, but everyone seemed to be out of control. I remember feeling quite frightened by it all. Even Father Wiltzius, our priest, whom everyone respected, couldn't calm us down. It was perhaps too soon after the war to forgive the suffering, humiliation and damage we had endured at the hands of the Nazis. The wounds were still fresh in our hearts and we just couldn't forget. Still, it was a shameful episode, but time, happily, is a great healer.

When we arrived back home in the evening we did nothing but talk about that unforgettable day. The Dancing Procession of 1945 went on record as a day to remember not only in the annals of the Olingen band but also in the history of the country itself.

The memorable year of 1945 saw the dawn of a new era for Luxembourg, a time of reconstruction all over the country. For me, leaving home to study in Luxembourg City, it became a time for hard work and those happy days 'On the other bank of the Syr' had come to an end.

Printed in the United Kingdom
by Lightning Source UK Ltd.
101695UKS00001B/208